Advance Praise for
Funds to the Rescue: 101 Fundraising Ideas for Humane and Animal Rescue Groups

"Fund raising is a challenge for those of us working to help the animals. *Funds to the Rescue* is practical and creative. Susan has done all the work letting the reader know what's involved with each idea—costs, planning time and how many people it takes to get them done. This book is a valuable resource for both start ups and established groups. I am planning to recommend it to students who attend workshops at Best Friends Animal Society and to the animal community at large."

> – Faith Maloney
> Animal Care Consultant,
> Best Friends Animal Society, www.BestFriends.org

Just about every non-profit rescue group understands the importance of fundraising. But many books don't give you specific and straight-forward ideas for pet-oriented fundraisers. With *Funds to the Rescue*, Susan Daffron offers honest advice about fundraising and then serves up 101 ideas that range from simple to complex fundraisers.

> – Holly Sizemore
> Executive Director, No More Homeless Pets in Utah
> www.UtahPets.org

"The tips that Susan offers in *Funds to the Rescue* are real, successful, and proven fundraising efforts that are doable by all. Susan shows many secrets on how to create long-lasting, sustainable relationships that are meaningful for both the givers and the receivers. For anyone who cares about animals, *Funds to the Rescue* is *the* best book to get to start saving lives today."

> – Casey Golden
> Founder and CEO of Small Act Network,
> co-author of *Do Your Giving While You're Living*

This book represents a great way to tackle fundraising in a contemporary setting and by removing the fear factor. Americans love animals and they will respond generously if you ask them properly for their support. Learn lessons from tried-and-true successes and apply them now for your agency!

> – Robert Evans
> Founder & Managing Director
> EHL Consulting Group, www.ehlconsulting.com

"Anyone involved in raising funds should read *Funds to the Rescue*! Susan doesn't just provide great ideas for raising funds, she lays out a complete, easy-to-follow framework for developing long-term, effective fundraising strategies that really work."

> – Ron Flavin
> Grants Access
> www.grantsaccess.com

"Whether you are new to the field of fundraising or an experienced fundraiser looking for ideas to raise money for a nonprofit that supports animals, this is a must read book. In a breezy and enthusiastic style, Susan Daffron offers both an overview of fundraising skills and detailed examples of how to raise money to support your mission."

> – Jane B. Ford, Speaker, Writer, Teacher, Coach
> www.thejoypath.com

"Fundraising can be a daunting task. Susan Daffron makes it much less so by providing "keys" to fundraising, marketing strategies, and other important information to consider. She also provides 101 creative ideas for raising funds, which include a rating system showing each idea's level of difficulty, planning time, up front cost, and volunteer resources required. A great resource for fundraising."

> – Lee Wlodarczyk
> Fundraising & Events Chairperson
> Tails of the Tundra Siberian Husky Rescue
> www.siberescue.com

I think this book is a great practical guide to assist even the most novice fundraiser. I believe that someone who is interested in advancing the cause of animal rescue can pick up this book and instantly begin both driving the critical messages and gaining needed funding to advance the mission. Congrats on what is a great book for helping Main Street gather it's resources for our animal friends.

> – John Brothers
> Principal, Cuidiu Consulting
> www.cuidiuconsulting.com

"Armed with the information in *Funds to the Rescue,* you'll never run out of ideas for your next fundraiser or "friend raiser." When you read Susan Daffron's Funds to the Rescue, you collect dozens of ideas you'll be eager to try or adapt for your organization.

> – Karen Eber Davis
> Karen Eber Davis Consulting
> www.kedconsult.com

Funds to the Rescue is a must-have for any animal rescue organization! While most books provide tips for raising money for your cause, they don't give you specific ideas for pet-oriented fundraisers. Susan Daffron offers solid advice about fundraising and then serves up 101 great ideas that range from simple to complex fundraisers.

> – Kristine Parkes
> CFRE of Krisp Communications
> http://www.krispcommunications.com

"I loved *Funds to the Rescue*! It's easy to read, very informative and creative. It's a great reference book that any non-profit can keep on their shelves to refer to over and over again."

> – Lana Wechsler
> Volunteer Coordinator, Paws For Patients
> New York-Presbyterian
> The University Hospital of Columbia and Cornell

"I love this book and the way Susan Daffron has empowered us all to make a bigger difference to our animals. *Funds to the Rescue* is thorough and innovative. It offers time-tested solutions and ideas for people who care. Susan gives us the stats, the encouragement and the ways to make a bigger difference. For our animal related causes. there is indeed something for every type of humane organization."

- Patty DeDominic,
  Business Coach, DeDominic & Associates
  Member of the Board of Directors,
  the Jane Goodall Institute USA
  www.dedominic.com

Funds to the Rescue

101 Fundraising Ideas for Humane and Animal Rescue Groups

Susan C. Daffron

Logical Expressions, Inc.
www.LogicalExpressions.com

ISBN: 978-0-9749245-9-5
Library of Congress Control Number: 2009905962

Contents

→ *Section 1* ←

The Hows and Whys of Fundraising

As the founder of the National Association of Pet Rescue Professionals (NAPRP), almost every day I talk to people involved in helping homeless animals. Virtually every rescue group is started by people with the best intentions. Some organizations thrive and save literally thousands of homeless pets every year; however, many animal shelters, humane and rescue groups struggle to raise money. In some cases, they are actually just a few dollars away from folding. Often people seem to think that "if I only could get that grant" everything will be just perfect!

Rescue groups that continue to struggle year after year often treat their organization like a hobby. They may set up occasional, haphazard, or scattershot fundraising efforts and become frustrated with the results. Non-profit does not mean no money. You need money to survive. People often make excuses: "the economy stinks" or "I can't think of an easy fundraiser." In these cases, eventually the founders get burned out and the organization folds. But the real losers are the animals that are no longer being helped.

It doesn't have to be that way. Fundraising is not new and countless humane organizations have figured out ways to successfully raise money for the animals, no matter what economic indicators are doing. The reality is that even during the Great Depression, some people still had money and some businesses actually did quite well.

In my case, about eight years before I founded NAPRP, I was involved with a small, private, local humane society, first as a volunteer, then an employee, and finally as a member of the board of directors. As the head of public relations, I helped organize and produce fundraisers, dealt with media, and created countless designs and artwork.

Later I consulted with other groups somewhat informally. During that time, I kept seeing the same problems cropping up over and over again. I realized I could help more groups if I formed a national organization. Now the National Association of Pet Rescue Professionals offers tools and information to help rescue groups raise more money and save more lives. Naturally, successful fundraising is one of the things we discuss a lot.

When fundraising works, it's a whole lot of fun and incredibly satisfying. You can see your effort quickly produce tangible results for the animals. This book is designed to give you some of the basics on getting started with fundraising and then gives you 101 ideas for animal-related fundraisers. To find these ideas, I scoured magazines, news sites, and the Internet to locate the coolest ideas people have thought up to help raise money for the animals.

Among the fundraising ideas you'll find in this book:

- How one humane society laughed themselves all the way to $43,000 with a fun comedy fundraiser.

- How working with restaurants can net big profits, like the shelter that told everyone to "Eat for Pete" (who is a very cute dog, by the way).

- How you can creatively ask for money using a simple letter-writing campaign instead of a bake sale, picnic, or dog walk. An SPCA made $980 the first day they used this tip.

- How to use the power of "small change" to your advantage. A few pennies can turn into a lot of dough!

- How to use nothing more than card stock and your printer for a super-quick and easy fundraiser.

- And 95 more. Armed with these 101, you'll never struggle to think up another fundraising idea again!

The introduction to fundraising at the beginning of this book and the 101 fundraising ideas give you a lot of food for thought, but I encourage you to learn more. The more complex the fundraiser, the more research you should do and the farther ahead you should plan. Don't be afraid to check out a lot of books from the library or even contact other charitable groups for advice. With a bit of extra research and advance planning, you may be able to avoid mistakes and earn more money!

Keys to Successful Fundraising

Fundraising doesn't have to be difficult; the key to successful fundraising is to raise money from a broad base of people. Although I mentioned that it seems like many organizations are stuck on getting grants, grants are not a long-term solution. Many grants are tied to one-time projects, such as improvements to a facility. Obviously grants are fantastic, but for basic day-to-day expenses you need to get a fundraising program in place.

In addition to the obvious advantage of bringing in more money, your fundraising efforts also have some side benefits. When you connect with people, you begin to establish a base of support for your organization—often more than financial—that you can draw upon for years to come. Donors may become members and often volunteers, as well. If there is a natural disaster or problem, your cadre of supporters will be the first people to come to your aid.

Don't underestimate the value of creating long-term relationships. In the "for-profit" business world, companies consider the "lifetime value" of a customer. The principles behind the lifetime value of a customer are actually quite simple and apply to connections in the non-profit world as well.

From a business standpoint, in order to calculate what a customer means to a business, time has to be included in the equation, because many customers will return. For example, suppose you own a hardware store. In 1999 a customer named Fred walks in and buys a $29 widget. Six months later in 2000, he sees an ad for your store, comes back in and purchases a mega-widget for $59. In 2001, he gets a postcard from you and buys a micro-widget for $109. Sometime in 2002, he moves out of state and you don't hear from him again (i.e. he's no longer a customer). Fred buys a total of $197 of merchandise from you over the course of three years. The average sale was $65 ($197 divided by 3). The key is that Fred's patronage is worth way more than that initial $29 sale.

In much the same way, many novice fundraisers focus so much on "getting more donations" that they don't consider what a simple contact can mean to the donor relationship over time. Perhaps you hold a fundraiser and it doesn't seem to do very well. You only get $100 in donations from 10 people. If you just grab the $10 and move on, you've missed a huge opportunity. What if you also take the time to ask each donor if you may add him or her to your newsletter list? Those people who donated $10 then receive a newsletter a week later asking people to sponsor a dog for $25/month for a year. If even one of those $10 donors signs up, you've now transformed that $10 contact into $300. If you follow up at the end of the year and the donor renews, the $10 that seemed like such a "failure" to begin with may have a tremendous "lifetime value" impact.

There's an old saying in business that it's always easier to sell to an existing customer. The same is true with donors. If you treat them well, past donors can be future donors.

In addition to helping you establish relationships, fundraising also gives you incredible opportunities for great publicity. Local media are dying for stories, so don't be lax about sending out a press release. Not every day is a "big" news day and people love human-interest stories. Puppies, kittens, bunnies, and other critters make for great TV. All this publicity increases community awareness of your organization and introduces you to other people who may want to help.

A recent ZooToo.com survey showed that 80% of people don't know where their local animal shelter is. Every community has animal lovers. It's vital to tell them where you are and what you're up to.

When you have fundraisers, you have an incredible opportunity to tell the media what you are doing. You have at least three (sometimes more) opportunities for publicity for everything you do:

1. **Before the event:** tell them what you are doing and when it's happening.

2. **During the event:** get someone to cover it. Or tell a story about someone affected by the fundraiser. ("Fido got adopted *and* a new Nylabone; we're thrilled!")

3. **After the event:** do a press release describing the results and thanking everyone involved.

When it comes to the media, an "event" doesn't necessarily mean something big at a particular time, like a dog walk. It can be something much simpler or smaller, such as a letter-writing campaign or product sales. The bottom line is to always tell the media what you are doing.

When it comes to fundraising, you should line up many different events to give potential donors multiple ways to get involved in your organization. For example, some donors are hands-off and just want to send money. Those people may respond to direct mail or an online donation opportunity. Other donors want to engage with your organization. They may get more excited about live events. Do both for the best results. Different people respond to different things.

Raising money for your organization is a big job, so don't try to take on every fundraising task yourself. Enlist other people to help and delegate tasks to them. Trying to do everything yourself is a sure-fire recipe for burnout.

Fundraising Statistics

When the economy goes downhill, there's a tendency to think, "nobody is donating" to anything. If you listen to the media, you might think nobody has any money to buy anything, much less donate. Even in a recession, people buy things and donate to causes they care about. Animal lovers don't suddenly *not* care about critters anymore.

In fact, the latest donor research from Campbell Rinker, a nonprofit marketing research firm in Santa Maria, California, shows that quite a bit of money is donated even during a recession.

According to the 2008 Campbell Rinker DonorPulse survey (http://www.afpnet.org/research_and_statistics/fundraising_research):

- Thirty-seven percent of charitable households gave more than $1,000 in 2007, including giving to places of worship.

- The average amount donated by charitable households in 2007 was $2,140, of which $940 went to places of worship.

- Donors are very likely (76%) to have given non-cash gifts of $25 or more to charity in the previous year.

- A majority (52%) have volunteered at least eight hours of time in the last year.

- A majority (56%) provided regular ongoing gifts to at least one charity in the last year.

- Only 10% of donors have a will, trust, or estate plan that includes a contribution to a non-profit organization.

That means that about half of the charitable money pool is available to you, as an animal organization. Religious organizations such as churches and other houses of worship always get the most donations; I'll talk more on what you can learn from religious organizations in another section. Also note that more than 50% of people volunteered their time. That's a big deal. After all, not all donations are financial. People will volunteer, even in a bad economy! The fact that only 10% of people have set up a will or estate plan is an opportunity for you as well. Don't forget that many baby boomers are animal lovers; encourage them to include your organization in their estate planning.

Donors were asked which type of contact prompted them to donate in 2007. Fundraising events and letters greatly surpassed other types of contact. Even with all the hoopla surrounding the Web and other media, these standbys still have an amazing ability to pull in donor dollars. So don't feel like a letter-writing campaign is too "boring." A simple letter can be incredibly effective.

Percentage of donors giving:

- Fundraising event 39%

- Letter 37%

- Telephone call 20%

- Workplace campaign 20%

- Something in a magazine, newspaper, or newsletter 13%
- Something on a Website 11%
- Something on television 11%
- Email 11%
- Something on the radio 9%
- None of the above 23%

Most business and non-profit experts seem to agree that the decisions organizations make during a recession actually have more influence on what happens than the recession itself. Right now, many businesses and non-profits are doing just fine. The key is to not panic but focus on the fundamentals of your business, such as marketing and fundraising. The dollars are out there and there's no reason they shouldn't go to you!

Keeping it Legal

Before I offer any more information on fundraising, I'd like to encourage you to research the laws in your area that relate to fundraising. As a non-profit organization, you need to consider the legal and tax implications of your activities. Most states regulate fundraising and you need to make sure that when people donate to your cause, they know what *is* and *is not* deductible.

When it comes to charitable contributions, cash, property and certain expenses can be deducted. But contributions that you receive in return for a service, product or other benefit, like a membership fee, are generally only partially deductible. On your fundraiser, you need to be very clear about how much of the donation is actually deductible. For example, if you put on a fundraising play for $20/seat, you have provided a service, so for donors it is only partially deductible. Talk to your accountant, and make sure your receipts clearly state in dollars how much the donor may use as a deduction on his tax return.

You also should check with your state about charitable solicitation laws. These laws are designed to protect donors from fraud. In most states, charities must register (see URS information below) and describe their fundraising activities. Generally they must file documents and pay an administrative fee.

This Web site:

http://www.multistatefiling.org/.

includes the Unified Registration Statement (URS) and a lot of information about registration. The URS form is accepted in 35 states and the District of Columbia. A few states don't require registration at all and three require registration, but don't use the URS.

According to the site, "The URS is an alternative to filing all of the respective registration forms produced by each of the cooperating states. In those states, a registering non-profit may use either the state form or the URS. Thus, the URS proves most useful to non-profits soliciting regionally or nationally and, therefore, subject to the registration laws of multiple states. But the URS may be used by any non-profit that is registering in a state accepting it."

The bottom line is that before you go forth and fundraise, get all the legal stuff handled first.

Marketing Basics

Honing Your Message

Successful fundraising involves getting your message out to the community and raising money so you can help animals. But in an increasingly cluttered and noisy world, you should make sure you have your message in place before you start.

In many communities, some groups struggle for donations simply because no one knows who they are, or because they are being confused with another animal-related organization. (This problem happens far more frequently than people think!)

Your job is to differentiate yourself and make your group memorable so people understand what you are doing to help animals. Remember the TV show "Cheers"? It was the bar you could go to where "everybody knows your name." In marketing circles, the "Cheers" secret to success is called "top-of-mind awareness." Getting donations is a lot easier if everybody in town already knows you!

To achieve top-of-mind awareness, you have to set yourself apart from the sea of charities, services, and businesses that are competing for the attention of your potential donors. Every day people are bombarded with countless marketing messages, so cutting through the clutter can be a challenge.

The key to rising above the general noise level is to create a consistent, distinctive message that resonates with your potential adopters and donors. Best Friends Animal Society is a great example of a group that has made itself distinctive. They have been using the No More Homeless Pets tagline for years. I'm guessing they have continued to use it because it works.

Everyone knows who they are, even though the sanctuary is located in the middle of rural Utah.

One of my favorite books for brainstorming ideas is called *POP: Stand Out in Any Crowd* by Sam Horn. In it, she suggests that your message needs to be "Purposeful, Original, and Pithy." Talk to your volunteers, staff, donors, or even people on the street and ask them about your organization. Don't settle for "the animal shelter in town." Come up with a unique identity or tagline that really says who you are and what you are trying to do. Then use it everywhere!

The Marketing Funnel Applied to Fundraising

In the business marketing world, sometimes you hear the term "marketing funnel." Although I've never seen it addressed specifically in the context of fundraising, the concept of a marketing funnel does apply.

Imagine the shape of a funnel. The top of the funnel is wide and the bottom is narrow. Prospective donors move from the top of the funnel to the bottom as they experience more of what you offer and become more involved.

The top represents people who know you exist and potentially will donate. Sure, everyone in the whole world could be a potential donor, but it's not exactly reasonable to expect that. Donors need to know you and need to have had some contact.

So at the top of your marketing funnel are "leads." These are people who have visited your Web site, seen one of your ads, driven by your location and seen your sign, read about you in the newspaper, or had some other type of minimal free contact with your organization. They haven't engaged with your organization yet, but they are aware that you exist.

Some percentage of that group may then engage in some way. They might sign up for you newsletter on your Web site, take a free dog-training class, or attend a fundraising event.

Now that these people have had contact with you and experienced your organization, trust begins to develop, so they may increase their contact. This group may adopt a pet from you, become a member, or volunteer for your organization.

Dedicated volunteers or people who have felt appreciated in some way may opt to increase their contribution level or participation. Later, they may become major donors or even include you in their estate planning.

Marketing Funnel
Applied to Fundraising

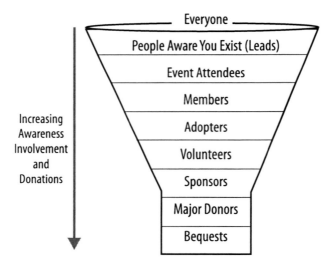

Everyone

People Aware You Exist (Leads)

Event Attendees

Members

Adopters

Volunteers

Sponsors

Major Donors

Bequests

Increasing Awareness Involvement and Donations

Money doesn't magically appear. The reason the marketing funnel concept is important is that it helps you realize that most donations don't "come out of nowhere." People need to have contact with you multiple times before they know and trust you enough to make a donation. Small donations often lead to big donations down the line. People don't think to donate, so you need to remind them. You have to ask for money.

If you are just getting started it may seem like it will take forever for anyone to find out that you exist. The least expensive form of marketing is word-of-mouth. An easy way to begin getting the word out is to start with the people you know. Talk to your friends, volunteers, and the initial organizers of your group. Have people write down names of people they know who can be asked for money. Almost inevitably someone knows someone who just happens to have a lot of money. See if they like animals. Remember, it never hurts to ask!

Where's the Money?

In general, the majority of donations tends to come from individuals; however, corporations, foundations or bequests are other sources. The best plan is to gather a wide range of supporters from as many areas as you can. Again, you can think about that funnel concept, but this time upside down. A traditional way to look at donations is referred to as the "Pyramid of Giving," which shows that usually the largest donations come from a small amount of donors.

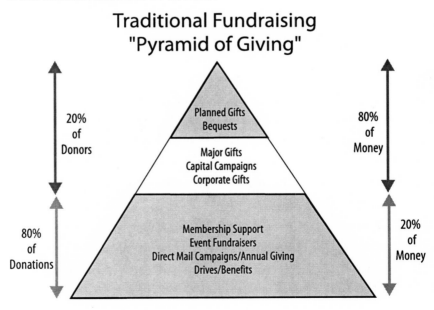

Fewer large businesses exist than individual donors, but the businesses may be in a position to give you larger donations.

Be creative and consider that money isn't the only type of donation you can receive from a business. If you know someone at a radio station, for example, see if you can get donated airtime. Media sponsors can be vital to the success of your event.

When you are planning your fundraising strategy remember that you aren't the only charitable organization out there—competition for donation dollars definitely exists. As I mentioned earlier, the largest percentage of charitable donations goes to religious organizations. Yes, you may have adorable fuzzy critters that you want to help, but it's hard to compete with someone's faith, so don't even try.

Even though you may not be able to offer eternal salvation as a benefit to joining your organization, you can learn a lot from how religious organizations raise funds. Yes, they may have God on their side, but houses of worship also have some real marketing advantages. Stop and think about a few of the reasons why religious organizations get the most donations.

First, the religious equivalent to your membership is parishioners. Churches and other houses of worship have their parishioners as a captive audience once a week. A house of worship has 52 opportunities to ask for money. If your donors hear from you only once a year for an annual appeal, no wonder you aren't getting as many dollars as the church or synagogue across the street. Fundraising is just like marketing in that you need to make a certain number of contacts with people for them to remember that you exist.

Religious organizations also ask everybody for money; they don't screen by perceived income. Yet many shelters don't ask people dropping off animals for a donation "because if they can't afford an animal, we shouldn't make them feel worse by asking for a donation." Why not? You're about to take care of their animal. Statistically, people in all income brackets donate to charitable causes.

Consider tithing, which some religious organizations use as a way to raise money consistently. Do you have type of regular giving options? (Give $10/month to sponsor an animal.) If not, you should. If you're a member of a congregation, notice what the organization does to encourage you to give. Some religious organizations have literally centuries of experience in raising a lot of money, so learn from their example!

Cause-Related Marketing

As you develop fundraisers, consider how you can work with other groups or businesses to create win-win partnerships. Many companies are actively looking to partner with non-profits in an effort to raise visibility and appeal to consumers. If a business aligns itself with a non-profit, it can make them look good in the eyes of their customers.

In fact, studies have shown that people are more likely to buy products from companies that associate themselves with good causes. The "for-profit" world knows all about this trend, so many companies are actively seeking partnerships. The bottom line: they need you!

The term "cause marketing" is a big buzzword in business these days. Research by Duke University and a cause-marketing agency called Cone shows that by associating themselves with a charitable cause, businesses can increase awareness of their brand and improve their sales. In fact, the study showed that the people who participated in the survey actually could recall both the specific cause and the product being advertised. In a world with an overwhelming and ever-increasing number of marketing messages, studies like that are a big deal in corporate America.

The study should be a big deal to you too! Use this cause-marketing trend to your advantage. Spend some time brainstorming some of the businesses you might be able to partner with to raise funds.

Assembling Your Team

There's No "I" in Team

As I mentioned, fundraising is a big job, and unless you want to make yourself crazy, you should not take it on yourself. You need help, so one of the first steps to effective fundraising is finding people to add to your merry band of fundraisers!

By setting up a team, you can leverage other people's talents and turn them into money to help the animals. You can't be good at everything, so your goal is to find people who love animals but are talented in areas where you are not. For example, you may need graphic support to create flyers for an event. I'm a writer and graphic artist, so in my years of volunteering, I was constantly recruited for my abilities in these areas. In contrast, my husband is a fantastic programmer, but the big joke at our house is that he can draw anything as long as it's a pig. (He's not someone you want on your Pictionary team!)

Find out what skills exist among your cadre of volunteers and supporters. Talk to people who are involved in your group in one way or another. Maybe they are people who have adopted pets from you or donated in the past. You can volunteer at an animal shelter with someone for months and never learn what she does at her day job. Chatting with someone walking a dog during lunch hour can be revealing. Lawyers, artists, writers, accountants, and other extremely skilled people may be a lot closer than you think!

It should go without saying, but when you are talking to people about fundraising, make it sound fun. Saying, "If we don't raise $5,000, we're doomed" does not make the process sound fun. It just makes you sound desperate. People volunteer out of love for and dedication to the animals. Don't turn volunteer time into drudgery. After all, many of them already have a regular job. Don't make helping your organization so arduous that you drive people away. People don't need another job!

Instead, focus on the benefits of working with you. Fundraising can be extremely satisfying because often you get tangible results quickly. It's exciting to work on something you really believe in. People enjoy working with other people who share their interests. For someone who has taken a tedious job to pay the bills, the boring day job may not offer the type of satisfaction that working with animals offers.

Because setting up events and other complex fundraisers can be a big undertaking, it's ideal if you can find people who have some type of past experience to draw upon. Even if you don't have the experience yourself, you may be able to find other people who have set up the same type of fundraiser. I remember a number of occasions when people walked into our animal shelter and said, "I just moved to the area. I have experience in fundraising, and I'd like to help." Do not EVER be "too busy" to talk to someone like this if they happen to wander through your door. Experienced volunteers like this are rare, so treat them well.

Having an incredibly experienced person come through your door is admittedly unusual, but finding volunteers doesn't have to be an overwhelming task. It is possible to find and keep great volunteers. If you are just starting out and don't have many contacts to draw upon for volunteers, consider talking to your local college. Students sometimes have more time and energy to volunteer than people who work long hours at a job. Point out that listing volunteer activities is a great addition to their resume. Creative students sometimes even incorporate their volunteer time into class projects or requirements.

Retirees are another often-overlooked volunteer group. Many older adults have extra time they are willing to devote to a cause they believe in. Talk to the senior center or organization in your town. Some areas also have volunteer networks that match volunteers with organizations that need them. Online, you can find the virtual equivalent: volunteer-match Web sites. Sign up your organization to make it easy for people to find you when they want to volunteer.

If you can't find a lot of people with fundraising experience to join your team, don't be afraid to contact other groups to find out about their fundraising experience. People love talking about their passion and often are willing to offer advice if you ask nicely. Another alternative is to look into a professional fundraising consultant to work with you. On a really large, important fundraiser, having the benefit of experience can make up for the fee or percentage charged.

Working with Volunteers

Volunteers are the lifeblood of your organization, so once you have them, you should treat them well. Just as with employees, a long-term volunteer has training and information that is incredibly valuable. If you keep volunteers happy, often you can count on the same group of volunteers to help you year after year.

For many years, the small town I live in has held a summer music festival. There are people who have volunteered for this charitable event for decades. Some people schedule their summer vacation here so that they can volunteer. (Imagine that—people volunteering for you on their vacation!) As you can imagine, a music festival is a big undertaking, but these long-term volunteers already know the ropes. Everything from music and concessions, to erecting the gigantic tent, is coordinated by people who have done it many times.

Many people are extremely busy; often families have two working parents, so they don't have much spare time. You may have to recruit more volunteers than in the past because each individual has fewer hours to give.

Spreading out the workload is also important because volunteers come and go. Even well run volunteer programs have a high turnover rate, so you should do everything you can to retain as many of your volunteers as possible.

Watch out for over-zealous volunteers who put in long hours. It's obviously extremely tempting to let these hard workers do a lot for you. But be careful; almost without exception these "power" volunteers burn out and leave. Instead, start them out slowly and build on success. You never want to be in the situation where only three or four people are stuck doing everything on every fundraiser because everyone else burned out. Distribute the work as evenly as possible and try to give people varying tasks so they don't get bored.

Again, you want to keep things fun. Many people volunteer for the social aspect of hanging out with other animal lovers, so think up reasons to bring people together. Instead of sending one volunteer home with a big pile of fundraising letters to mail, make it a fun "lick-and-stick" party. Have a potluck event at someone's house, where you get together to sign, fold, stuff, lick, and stick. Think of ways you can keep your group social. People make lasting friendships through volunteer activities. When your volunteers think of your group as a bunch of friends having fun helping the animals, you know you're on the right track!

It should go without saying that you must thank and reward your volunteers. In your quest to get a fundraiser going, it can be easy to forget little things like "thank you." Make each and every volunteer feel special. After all, they are giving you their time and skill for free. Never devalue the importance of their generosity to your organization! Some organizations give away small tokens of appreciation, such as certificates or t-shirts, but don't underestimate the power of just saying, "you did a really good job and we appreciate it!"

Along with accomplishing tasks, think of reasons to get together and just chat about how things are going. Not everything has to be an "official meeting." Keeping people in the loop on the big picture gives them a stake in the outcome of your fundraising activities.

Most people volunteer because they want to make a difference. Always make sure they know that they have!

Fundraising Planning

Create a Fundraising Calendar

The old saying that nothing happens without a plan is particularly true when it comes to fundraising. You can't create a realistic budget if you don't know where your money is coming from and when it's coming in.

The first step is to set up a fundraising calendar. Make a list of all your proposed fundraising activities and then share it with your volunteers. Each activity will require its own plan. Additionally, many communities have events calendars that are printed far in advance, so you want to make sure your events are on them.

Planning ahead is vital to your organization and your sanity. I recommend that you place all your big in-person events on the calendar first. Make sure they don't conflict with other events in your community and that you can get space at the venue you want. Most organizations have only one or two big events, so try to space them six months apart if possible. For example, you might have a dog walk in the summer and a black-tie New Year's Eve event in the winter. Try to plan your fundraisers as far in advance as you can.

Now fill in smaller events for other months. For example, you might do a letter-writing campaign in February. This activity will require far fewer volunteers than the dog walk. Even though it's no less important, it requires fewer resources.

Make sure you set up specific dates. It's obvious that you need to pick a date for an event, but even smaller things like that letter-writing campaign needs to have a clear target date, or it won't get done. Also take your volunteers' schedules into account. If you have a lot of student volunteers, they may have more time in the summer. Conversely, if many of your volunteers are on vacation in the summer, you may not want to schedule a big event then.

It's better to have fewer, more powerful, fundraisers than a bunch of ineffective ones. For one thing, you don't want to burn out your volunteers, but you don't want to tap out your donors, either. If you have too many fundraisers going on, people may hesitate to give money. No one likes to be constantly nagged to give, after all.

You also will need to set a budget for your fundraising activities. Obviously some fundraisers incur more costs, so keep an eye on your cash flow situation. Money—both incoming and outgoing—is another good reason to space your fundraising activities throughout the year.

Make sure you keep track of what worked and what didn't from year to year. Fundraising is all about raising the most money with the least amount of resources (whether volunteer or financial). Some fundraisers may be so much effort that even though everyone loves them, they are just too much work. Again, you don't want to burn out your volunteers or employees.

With that said, when it comes to looking at the results of a fundraiser, do consider community awareness as well. Sometimes it takes a few years for an event to "get traction" and really start to make money. If something seemed like a big success among attendees but didn't make a whole lot of money, don't reject it out-of-hand. It may just need a little more time to become a blockbuster.

Particularly with events, sometimes your fundraising effort can be about a lot more than just raising money. Make your event about connecting with your supporters for a great cause: animals! Building a community of support yields big dividends in the long run.

Once you have some experience under your belt, you can make better choices. For example, the first time you ask a retailer or supplier for a donation or a service, you don't know what they'll be like to work with. In fact, you may not even know what questions you need to ask. Next time, it will be easier and you'll know which folks are great to work with and which ones you should avoid.

Offering Many Ways to Donate

Part of creating a broad-based fundraising plan is offering many different ways for people to engage with your organization. Think about all the different ways and times people come in contact with you. Many of these interactions can result in a fundraising opportunity. For example:

- **Adoptions** - when someone adopts an animal, he is saving a life. It's probably one of the best times to make donating easy. Include a membership envelope in your adoption packet. Or just put a donation jar on the front counter.

- **Product Sales** (if you have a store) or Service (e.g. grooming) - Make sure people know that you are a non-profit. Products and services aren't deductible, but you have an opportunity to tell people how they *can* make a tax-deductible donation.

- **Events** - during events try to think of multiple ways you can make money. At a dog walk, include a bake sale as well. While doing a presentation on dog behavior, sell memberships at the back of the room.

- **Email/Online Donations** - read about online marketing techniques to draw more people to your Web site. Add a simple PayPal button so people can donate online. In every email newsletter, be sure to ask for a donation. Online marketing is a huge topic and beyond the scope of this book. Using social media tactics (Facebook, Twitter, MySpace) can be a great way to raise awareness as well.

- **Fundraising Letters** - direct mail is often overlooked in our Web 2.0 world, but it remains very effective.

- **Membership** - when someone becomes a member, it's a perfect opportunity to ask for an additional donation.

- **Annual Gifts** - some people regularly donate at Christmastime or other holidays. Keep track of people who come in at a certain time of year and mail them a letter to save them time.

- **Regular Sponsorship** - annual or monthly (sponsor an animal/cage) - people who visit your facility and engage with your animals may love seeing their name on a kennel. When someone comes in to walk dogs, tell them about your "Adopt-a-Kennel" program.

- **Memorials, Bequests, Life Insurance** - Make sure people know you offer these types of programs. Talk to estate planning lawyers and insurance agents in your area and ask if you can give them brochures.

- **Corporate Contributions** - If you partner with a company on an event, don't forget to ask for a donation from them. Often you'll be dealing with someone in a particular department. See if they can move your request "up the food chain."

Deciding on Fundraisers

If you spend any time flipping through the ideas in this book, you may realize that there's no shortage of creative ways to make money. Of course, the flip side is that you might have so many options, you don't know which ones to choose!

Here are a few thoughts on selecting a fundraiser. First, don't select a fundraising project just because you read that it made a lot of money or a friend of a friend said it's the "best" idea ever. Do some research before you dive in. Also consider your team and the amount of time you have. Be realistic. Has anyone on your team done this particular type of fundraiser before? If not, you should do even more research to find out exactly what's involved and how much money you can realistically earn, given the resources you have available.

The ideas in this book range from the simple to the complex. When I could, I tried to include dollar figures from actual humane groups who used the idea. But don't think those numbers are gospel. The groups I featured range widely in size from large humane organizations like the Denver Dumb Friends League to tiny breed-specific dog rescues. The amount of money you can make depends on the size of your group, the community, and a hundred other variables.

When you have decided on a fundraising tactic, consider the amount of money you need to earn, the size of your staff and volunteers and the amount of time you want to devote to the effort. For example, suppose you want to raise $1,000 in the next month and you have 20 people willing to help. That would be $50/person. If you have something like a quilt to raffle off, each person could commit to selling $50 worth of tickets. If each volunteer sells 50 $1 tickets, you reach the goal. Or you could price the tickets at $2, so each person has to sell only 25.

Always take any up-front expenses into account in your calculations. Some classic fundraisers, like selling candy or other products, require an up-front purchase of product. Make sure you can cover your costs. If people aren't excited about selling candy, odds are good they won't do a good job. Select a fundraising activity that people enjoy and, ideally, that relates to your mission. Animal people undoubtedly will be more excited about selling animal-related stuff than candy bars!

Stay on the lookout for new, creative ideas. It's easy to get "stuck in a rut" and stay with the same tried-and-true techniques over the years. Unfortunately, long-term volunteers (and you) may end up simply getting bored with the same old-same old. Check out the ideas in this book and share them with your team. Do any of them sound really fun? If so, do your research and boldly try them out! Odds are good you might have more fun and even make more money!

Setting Goals and Objectives

After you have planned your overall fundraising strategy, you should set goals and objectives for each fundraising activity you plan to do. As I said, you need to get down to the nitty-gritty and start setting budgets and timelines.

For each fundraiser, you should include your financial goals and detail the reason for the fundraiser. For example, for your dog walk, you might say, "the Strut Your Mutt Dog Walk is designed to increase the awareness of Dog Rescue in Somewheretown and raise money for our spay/neuter coupon program. Our goal is to get 300 people to pay $20 to participate, which will raise $6000. We also plan to sell food and drink at the event, which will raise another $500."

Each fundraising activity should have a budget, in which you outline the money you plan to raise, along with the costs. Raising $6,500 at your dog walk sounds great, but you need to subtract your costs as well. So if you need to rent a facility, pay for a DJ or incur other costs, make sure you take them into account. Consider working with your accountant or bookkeeper to create a budgeting worksheet form you can reuse for each fundraiser.

Obviously, as you plan your goals and objectives, you'll be working with other people. However, don't let things get bogged down in a morass of bureaucracy. Sometimes at meetings, it can feel like you are trying to herd cats to get anyone to commit to doing anything.

Make sure your fundraising committees stay small and workable so you don't end up with 50 people in a room yelling at each other. Set an agenda for every meeting and remain on task. Create a workable organizational chart so that people at different levels have the authority to make decisions in their area.

Unless you have a really small organization, it's unlikely you will need to get approval from everyone on every decision. Also, remember that in the event of discord, somebody has to have the authority to have the last word, or nothing ever will happen on anything.

Create a Timeline

Along with your goals, you need to develop a timeline for your fundraiser. If it's an event, you need to work backward from the event date and schedule the tasks and activities that are necessary to make the event happen.

Be sure to take lead times into account. For example, if you are getting posters printed, you may need to get the artwork to the printer two weeks before the date you plan to hang them up around town. Then it may take two days for your volunteers to put them up, so you need to allow a total of 16 days.

Be sure to give everyone deadlines and stay on top of who is supposed to be doing what when. You should review your timeline frequently to make sure everything is happening on schedule. There are a lot of details to manage and the reality is that even the "best-laid plans often go awry." So as you manage your project, you may want to build in some "buffer" to help mitigate any surprises that occur during the fundraising process.

Assign Roles

As I mentioned, to pull off any fundraiser, you need to assign people to tasks and give them deadlines. You must hold your volunteers accountable for the things they have agreed to do. When you assign people tasks, ensure they stick to them.

A key to getting things done and keeping volunteers happy is to give them the "4 Ws and the H" that relate to the jobs to which they've been assigned. Journalists know that you have to include the "who, what, when, why, and how" to write a story. In much the same way, you need to clearly explain all the jobs involved in your fundraising effort. You need to figure out:

- Who is doing which task
- What that person needs to do to complete the task
- When the task needs to be completed
- Why the task is important to the big picture (everyone needs to know why they are raising the money!)
- How it needs to be done

When you have everyone on the same page, they start to "own" their task. One key to successful delegating is to avoid micromanaging people. Trust your team to do a good job. Assume people will do the right thing, until they don't. Then quickly find a replacement. Have back-up plans in mind in case someone drops the ball. Also, be sure to keep expanding your network. Ask volunteers if they have friends who might be able to help.

Always try to match volunteers' tasks to their skills. Don't try and force someone who hates accounting to keep track of finances, just because "we need that." When people offer to volunteer, consider asking them to fill out a questionnaire so you can find out their likes, dislikes, and skills. Although it's great if you can capitalize on someone's professional skills, realize that sometimes people want to do something (anything) else when volunteering.

If you are working with a number of volunteers, you'll probably need to form committees. Don't saddle one person with all the work. Try to pull together a wide range of people to work on a committee so they can draw on each other's strengths.

Don't put all your "numbers people" on one committee and all the "artsy" people on another. Mix it up a bit.

Speaking of numbers, you should make sure someone is in charge of keeping records of all the money that is coming in and going out. Yes, bookkeeping can be boring, but it must be done. Having a history of costs and income is also important, so you can see how things change (and possibly improve) from year to year.

Saying Thank You Is Vital

Saying thank you is an often-overlooked aspect of fundraising. You should take the time to recognize every contribution. Handwritten notes are best. It's important to make sure every donor and every volunteer is thanked.

If you're working with a lot of volunteers or receive a lot of donations all at once, it can seem arduous to write a whole lot of personal letters, but these thank-yous are important to long-term success. Unlike a job, for which someone has to go to work to get a paycheck, a volunteer doesn't *have* to volunteer. Donors receive pitches from many organizations; they don't have to donate to your cause. Make them feel special. After all, which group would you donate to—the one that sent a thank-you note, or the one that didn't?

Remember what I said about the lifetime value of a customer? In this case, your "customer" is a donor, and it's likely you'll be asking for his support again. Most non-profits receive donations from the same people year after year. They may be adopters, volunteers, relatives of employees or board members, or just people who have professed to believe in what you do. If you want to continue to get those funds, you need to stay in touch.

People need reasons to donate, so make sure you always tell people how their funds will be spent and then tell them what happened afterward. Let them know that because of their support for the Neuter is Cuter drive, you were able to meet your goal to "fix" 100 cats.

When you let people know what you're doing, they're more inclined to help. You aren't just saying, "We need money." Instead you're engaging people in your mission. (In this case, "We want to lower the number of cats coming into shelters.") Help people understand why you are doing what you're doing.

People love to feel appreciated. You can't say thank you too many times!

Final Thoughts

Although raising funds for your organization is a lot of work, the results are worth it. Effective fundraising helps you build a more successful and sustainable organization. Always remember that you are doing it to help the animals. If you don't have money, you can't help them!

If you're just starting out, the task of raising money and taking care of your animals at the same time can seem downright overwhelming. There is just so much need and it can be difficult not to become discouraged sometimes.

Take heart in the fact that things will get better over time. As more people learn about the great work you are doing, you'll attract more members and volunteers. With help, everything becomes easier. Each event you do and every fundraising activity you perform builds momentum. It's like a snowball rolling downhill; the farther it goes, the bigger it gets.

You need to try a lot of different things and see what works. Realize that it may take time for something to become a true success. Big events in particular often take time to ramp up to the point that they are serious moneymakers. Many times the amount of money earned from an event grows in small increments year after year, so give it time.

Here's an example of what not to do. When I was doing fundraising work for our local shelter, we put on a community event called the Bow Wow Pow Wow at the fairgrounds. Dubbed the "canine event of the season," we brought in vendors, had contests and really did it up. The first year, it didn't make much money. But by the second year, people were looking forward to it and the event made more money than it did the first year. It was also easier to put on the second time because we had the first year's experience to draw upon. Sadly, the event never really got to reach its potential. The management of the shelter changed and the event was never held again. Years later, people still ask me why it "went away."

The moral of this story is make a commitment to your fundraisers. If you do opt for a big event, don't bail out on it. Turn it into the type of event that people look forward to every year. Understand that it may take a few years before the event really starts to make a lot of money, so be patient and look at the long-term big picture.

Also don't discount the "little" fundraisers that can earn a lot of money with little effort. Probably the easiest fundraiser I ever did was the paw print fundraiser (which is mentioned in this book). Our costs were: one ream of paper, some of my time to design artwork and one volunteer going around to businesses with hearts, yet it made hundreds of dollars. Patrons of the businesses purchased a "paw print valentine" for a dollar. They were hung up on the walls of the establishments, so essentially the fundraiser advertised itself.

We copied that idea from the Muscular Dystrophy Association, which does a similar fundraiser on St. Patrick's Day in grocery stores throughout the country. Keep collecting fundraising ideas. It's easy to adapt someone else's fundraiser to benefit pets.

As you have more successes under your belt, consider expanding your planning beyond a year. Think about where you want to be in five or ten years. Start dreaming big. The money is out there, so go for it!

Now onward to the 101 ideas!

101
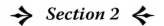
Fundraising Ideas

Now that you have some "big picture advice" on successful fundraising, it's time to forge ahead into the 101 ideas themselves. After each idea, you'll find ratings. Keep in mind that "1" is low and "5" is high.

Happy fundraising!

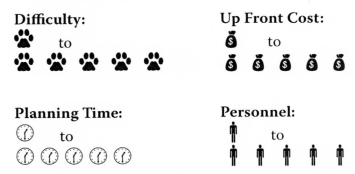

Difficulty: to

Up Front Cost: to

Planning Time: to

Personnel: to

1

Wishing or Hope Tree

During the holiday season an easy fundraiser is to put a tree in a high-traffic area such as a mall or busy office. Create paper ornaments to hang on the tree, naming donations you would like on each one. Donors remove an ornament and purchase the item they want to donate. Depending on the location of the tree, the gifts can be left under the tree or in a secured area.

A related idea (the "Hope Tree") is to put the name of an animal on each ornament instead of items to be donated. People donate money for the adoption fee, in effect "sponsoring" the animal. This allows a person (such as a senior citizen on a fixed income) who has enough money to own a pet, but not the up-front fee for vet care, to adopt. The Humane Educational Society in Tennessee set up a Hope Tree in 2007. The fundraiser raised awareness for the HES and news stories featured specific animals that had been waiting for adoption for a long time.

Level of...
- Difficulty =
- Planning Time =
- Upfront Costs =
- Personnel =

2

Have a Hair Ball

Feline rescues might consider having a "Hair Ball" like the one hosted by the Humane Society of Greater Dayton (Ohio). The group ran the fundraiser to raise money specifically for its feline programs. The event drew around 500 people and raised $36,000.

The Hair Ball was run in conjunction with local hair salons. Teams representing local Dayton-area salons participated in the event, which sported a "CAT-tastrophic" hairstyles theme. During the event, scantily clad people volunteered to dress up and model their new fabulous hairstyles for three minutes along a catwalk set up at a local club. Slinking and swaying to tunes, the models for each salon's team competed for prizes in categories such as Top Cat, Wild Cat, and Most Hair-Raising.

Level of...

- Difficulty = 🐾 🐾 🐾 🐾
- Planning Time = 🕐 🕐 🕐 🕐
- Upfront Costs = 💰 💰 💰
- Personnel = 👤 👤 👤 👤

3

Have a 5K Race

In the Northwest, the Seattle Animal Shelter has an annual "Furry 5K Fun Run and Walk" which draws around 2,300 participants and 1,000 dogs. Unlike a regular "dog walk," the 5K is a competitive road race. Dogs and their humans are awarded prizes and the event generates a lot of community spirit. All proceeds from the event go to veterinary care for sick, injured, immature, and abused animals in the shelter. The Furry 5K also attracts around 45 animal (and non-animal) vendors.

In 2007 the Somerset County Humane Society in Pennsylvania sponsored its first-ever "Hug a Friend 5K" run (and walk). In this case, money was raised through entry fees and the sale of t-shirts.

Setting up an event on the scale of the Furry 5K requires a lot of volunteers and planning. But the rewards both in community goodwill and fundraising can be considerable.

Level of...

- Difficulty = 🐾 🐾 🐾 🐾 🐾
- Planning Time = 🕐 🕐 🕐 🕐 🕐
- Upfront Costs = 💰 💰 💰 💰
- Personnel = 👤 👤 👤 👤 👤

4

Garage Sale Fundraiser

A garage sale is a fairly inexpensive way to make a little extra cash during good weather. Many groups make it an annual event. For example, in Lafayette, Louisiana, the Acadiana Humane Society holds an annual garage sale fundraiser every June. The process isn't difficult. First, write a press release soliciting donations for the "big sale" with a headline like, "Humane Society Seeks Donated Items for Garage Sale." Ask donors to bring their donations to your facility and if you have a volunteer with a big truck, offer to pick up big items such as furniture. (These things can sell for good money at the sale, so it's worth it to help donors get them to you!)

You also can make your garage sale about more than just the sale itself. The Humane Society of South Central Michigan in Battle Creek, Michigan has turned their garage sale into an all-day event. Their Pet-A-Pal-ooza fundraiser includes the garage sale, adoption opportunities, educational displays, training demonstrations, face painting for kids, refreshments, "paw readings" (by a non-psychic) and other fun activities.

Level of...

- Difficulty = 🐾 🐾 🐾
- Planning Time = 🕐 🕐 🕐
- Upfront Costs = 💰 💰
- Personnel = 👤 👤 👤 👤

5

Weight Pull with Kegs or Pumpkins

If your town has a microbrewery, you can partner with them to do a Canine Keg Pull. In Sandpoint, Idaho, this event has been raising money for the local animal shelter for many years and is one of the most talked-about events during the local Winter Carnival. (In fact, the original microbrewery is now long gone, but a nearby bar took over sponsorship of the event.)

In a keg pull, dogs are harnessed to empty beer kegs and timed as they pull the keg down a snow-covered track. Small dogs pull pony kegs. The fastest dogs win prizes. Funds are raised from entry fees and the sale of various dog-related products, such as bandannas and t-shirts.

An alternative to the keg pull is to pull pumpkins or bags of dog food. Sue Sternberg's Rondout Valley Animals for Adoption (RVAA) runs "Lug Nuts" weight-pulling events. Pumpkins are placed on plastic snow sleds and the dogs pull them using padded pulling harnesses. Because often the dogs most gifted at weight-pulling are the "muscle" and "bull" breeds and their mixes, Sternberg offers "Lug Nuts" as an educational event to show that pit bulls can participate in positive events.

Level of...

- Difficulty = 🐾 🐾 🐾
- Planning Time = 🕐 🕐 🕐 🕐
- Upfront Costs = 💰 💰 💰
- Personnel = 👤 👤 👤

6

Sell Catnip

If you have gardeners among your cadre of volunteers, encourage them to grow catnip. The plant is extremely easy to grow and dry. And of course, many cats just go nuts for catnip, so it's easy to sell it to the owners and friends of felines.

The cost to do this fundraiser is almost nothing. You can package "the 'nip" in little bags from the dollar store or if you have volunteers who sew, ask them to sew the bags. Dry the catnip, crumble it and put it in the bags.

Give the catnip a fun and special name. For example, photograph one of your cats, name him "Nick" and call your bag of catnip "Nick's 'Nip" on the label. Or use a play on words like Cat-a-Tonic, 8 Lives, or Hot Tin Roof Catnip.

Level of...

- Difficulty =
- Planning Time =
- Upfront Costs =
- Personnel =

7

Sell Bricks or Tiles

If you are doing a capital campaign for a new building or restoration project, consider selling a piece of the building to raise money. Work with an engraving company, landscape/ rock contractor, mason, tile artist or other company that can customize building materials and sell engraved rocks, bricks, or customized tiles. For example, each brick that makes up the building or walkway can be engraved with a donor's name. People like having their name immortalized, so bricks/tiles can be sold for $100 - $300 (sometimes more). People also will buy bricks for loved ones as a permanent memorial.

Once the building is complete, years later people will stop and look for their name and those of friends among the bricks. Building materials like bricks and tiles remain a permanent reminder of donations and the initial cost is not much more than the cost of the building materials, which you have to purchase anyway!

Level of...
- Difficulty = 🐾 🐾
- Planning Time = 🕐 🕐 🕐
- Upfront Costs = 💰 💰
- Personnel = 🧍 🧍

8

Affiliate Links

When it comes to fundraising, don't forget about your Web site. Many online programs give you a percentage of a sale if visitors to your site click a link to a merchant and buy something.

Called "affiliate programs," this arrangement benefits both your organization and the merchant who offers the product. They get the sale and you get a commission. You should sign up only for affiliate programs with merchants that sell products related to what you do. Big pet stores like www.PetSmart.com have affiliate programs; smaller companies do too. For example, we offer a 20% affiliate commission on our books for adoptive pet owners: *Happy Hound* (www.HappyHoundBook.com) and *Happy Tabby* (www.HappyTabbyBook.com).

Note that you will need someone with Web site knowledge to set up your links, but once they are set up, you shouldn't have to deal with it often.

New adopters always need "stuff" for their pets, so direct them to buy items through links on your site. It doesn't cost them any more than if they shopped directly on the site, but you can tell them that every click helps you, too!

Level of...
- Difficulty = 🐾 🐾 🐾
- Planning Time = 🕐 🕐
- Upfront Costs = 💰
- Personnel = 🧍

9

Get Used Vehicle Donations

If you have supporters who are into cars and auto repair, consider establishing a used vehicle donation program. Many people have cars or trucks that, for tax reasons, they would rather donate than sell.

As an example, a volunteer for the Anne Arundel County SPCA in Maryland ran a used-vehicle donation program by himself. He picked up vehicles from donors' residences, cleaned them up, repaired them and sold them through ads in the local paper. In 1997, the efforts of this one volunteer raised $40,000 for the SPCA. That's a lot of money for a bunch of old cars!

Level of...

- Difficulty = 🐾 🐾 🐾
- Planning Time = 🕐 🕐 🕐
- Upfront Costs = 💰
- Personnel = 👤 👤

10

Retriever Fundraiser

Do you run a retriever rescue? Consider having an exhibition or fundraiser that lets the dogs show their stuff. The first thing you need is a lot of tennis balls, so find an inexpensive source for them, such as a racquet club or a gym where used tennis balls are thrown away. Sometimes you can find large quantities of tennis balls for sale online as well. The second thing you need is to solicit cool donated prizes from vendors.

Once you have your collection of tennis balls, you need one or more dogs who *really* like to retrieve. Donors purchase the tennis balls, which have been numbered, and keep a ticket with their number on it. At the event the balls are dumped out all at once. A few tennis balls are launched and the dog commences retrieving.

Donors win prizes when the dog retrieves the ball with their number. You can use multiple dogs and/or offer multiple prizes with just one dog who retrieves really well. You may want to do a "dry run" to work out possible issues with different dog behaviors and locations. For example, when faced with that many tennis balls, some dogs will pick up multiple balls or pick up one and drop it without bringing the ball back to the human.

The G.R.E.A.T. (Golden Retriever Emergency Assistance Team) Rescue of NE Florida ran a Tennis Ball Bonanza fundraiser that used a variation on this theme. Because goldens love to swim, the group threw the numbered tennis balls into a swimming pool. Photos of the event on the GreatRescue.org Web site indicate that this "pool party" was fun for everyone, including "Maggie," the golden who took the plunge.

Level of...

- Difficulty = 🐾 🐾 🐾
- Planning Time = 🕐 🕐 🕐
- Upfront Costs = 💰 💰
- Personnel = 👤 👤 👤

11

Take the Plunge

In Hagerstown, Maryland, the Humane Society of Washington County raised money by convincing 114 people (who had to solicit pledges) to jump into the Potomac River on New Year's Day. Those who got the most pledges earned prizes, such as movie and ice-skating passes and mugs. Money also was earned through a bake sale and corporate sponsorship.

The Humane Society raised $6,000, which will be used to care for the animals. Many cities and towns that are near a body of water have some type of "polar bear plunge." If you can find enough nutty people who are willing to jump into freezing bodies of water, it's a fairly easy fundraiser that invariably gets press attention.

Level of...

- Difficulty = 🐾 🐾
- Planning Time = 🕐 🕐 🕐
- Upfront Costs = 💰 💰
- Personnel = 🧍 🧍 🧍

12

Run a Cooking Contest

Everyone likes food, so one way to get people out in droves is to entice them with a cooking contest. For example, you might run a "Fudge-o-Rama" where local chefs enter their most creative fudgy concoctions. Those in attendance or official "celebrity" judges can vote on the best ones and award prizes.

In the end, you sell the food and/or auction off the award-winning entries. The concept can work for almost any type of food. Chili cook-offs, pizza bakes, pie contests, and other baking-oriented events are popular.

Level of...

- Difficulty = 🐾 🐾
- Planning Time = 🕐 🕐 🕐
- Upfront Costs = 💰 💰
- Personnel = 🧍 🧍 🧍

13

Have a Wine Tasting

For the last five years, the Carver-Scott Humane Society in Minnesota has held a wine-tasting event called "Hound Dog Heaven." Tickets to the fundraiser cost $45 in advance or $50 at the door and attendees have the opportunity to "step back in time" to the 1950s with vintage décor, DJ-provided rock 'n' roll music and classic diner food. A local wine and spirits shop donates the wine. During the evening a silent auction is held featuring gifts donated by other local businesses and "friends of the animals."

Wine tastings can be popular and lucrative fundraisers, particularly if you partner with a local wine bar or spirits shop that is willing to provide the "goods" and possibly the venue.

Level of...

- Difficulty = 🐾 🐾 🐾
- Planning Time = 🕐 🕐 🕐 🕐
- Upfront Costs = 💰 💰 💰
- Personnel = 👤 👤 👤

14

Have a Fun Fest

The Vanderburgh Humane Society in Indiana puts on an annual Fido Walk & Fun Fest, which serves multiple purposes: it promotes the human-animal bond, increases awareness of the organization, and raises money for the many programs operated by the humane society.

Hundreds of pets and their humans "high-tail" it to the Fun Fest, which features pet-related vendors, dog shows, an off-leash park, contests for agility, and prizes for the top fundraisers. Money is raised through entry fees, dog wash fees, and pledges. Organizers hoped the 2007 event would raise $15,000 for the humane society. The registration form was placed on their Web site and those who raised more than $75 received a t-shirt.

Although planning a big event like this is a lot of work, it can be worth it as both a fundraiser and as an annual fun "animal celebration" that increases awareness of your organization's mission.

Level of...
- Difficulty = 🐾 🐾 🐾 🐾 🐾
- Planning Time = 🕐 🕐 🕐 🕐
- Upfront Costs = 💰 💰 💰 💰
- Personnel = 🧍 🧍 🧍 🧍 🧍

15

Silent Auction

A silent auction is a type of auction that doesn't require an auctioneer. Items up for bid are placed on tables with sheets of paper in front of them for a limited time.

People write their name and how much they are willing to pay for the item on the sheet. Other people sign up with higher bids. At the end of the time period, the sheets are collected and the person with the highest bid for each item gets to take it home.

The most difficult part of a silent auction is coming up with donated items. You'll have to start far in advance and recruit a number of people to help you solicit donations.

Possible items can be knick-knacks from gift stores, dinners at local restaurants, vacation trips from travel companies or services like housecleaning, tax preparation or car washes. You are limited only by your imagination and donor's generosity.

For example, in Alabama the Chilton County Humane Society held a silent auction. Bidding ran from 9 a.m. to 2 p.m. and some of the items up for bid included candlesticks, lamps, a Christmas centerpiece, wall hangings, free spay and neuter certificates from local veterinarian, free pet grooming, a large outdoor pet kennel, gift baskets, a free haircut and style, and a free steak dinner for two.

Level of...
- Difficulty = 🐾 🐾 🐾
- Planning Time = 🕐 🕐 🕐 🕐
- Upfront Costs = 💰 💰
- Personnel = 👤 👤 👤

16

Sponsor an Animal

You have animals, so one easy way to raise money is to have people "sponsor" a pet. Calculate how much it costs to feed a critter in your care and divide it out on a monthly, quarterly, semi-annual, or yearly basis.

Print flyers that explain what the sponsorship costs are and what they pay for. In exchange, each sponsor might get a certificate with a picture of the animal and his history. Businesses may be inclined to hang these on the wall to show that they support your organization and pets in the community.

A sponsorship program can be a compelling way to show people exactly where their money is going. The costs to you are basically just in time, paper, postage, and creativity.

Level of...

- Difficulty = 🐾 🐾
- Planning Time = 🕐 🕐
- Upfront Costs = 💰
- Personnel = 👤 👤

17

Arts and Crafts Fair

Many people are "crafty." When you get enough of them together, you have the makings for an Arts and Crafts fair. For this fundraiser, find a group of artists and crafters to make goods and then ask for a percentage of the money earned at the fair.

If you don't want to organize the event yourself, consider partnering with a local arts council or other art-related organization. After all, it's great advertising for them to say that part of the proceeds of the fair help the animals!

You also can partner with artists who are shown in galleries. Ask an artist if you can get a percentage of sales from a gallery show or ask him to donate an original piece to be raffled.

Level of...

- Difficulty = 🐾 🐾 🐾 🐾
- Planning Time = 🕐 🕐 🕐 🕐
- Upfront Costs = 💰 💰 💰
- Personnel = 👤 👤 👤 👤

18

Walk Naked

This fundraiser may sound like an urban legend, but it's true. In 1998, PAWS-itive Partners Humane Society in North Platte, Nebraska, made headlines with a promotion they called Walking Naked.

The mayor made a public promise to walk Naked down Main Street if the group managed to raise $5,000. It turned out Naked was a dog. The promotion actually raised $12,000, thanks to the tremendous amount of press it received.

You can try a similar promotion with terms like topless, no pants, underpants, and so forth. Anything that causes a little raise of the eyebrows probably will net you some easy press!

Just make sure that the individual wearing no pants, no top, or no underpants is not a human.

Level of...
- Difficulty = 🐾 🐾 🐾
- Planning Time = 🕐 🕐
- Upfront Costs = 💰
- Personnel = 🧍 🧍

19

Exclusive Shopping Spree

The Animal Shelter, Inc. of Sterling, Massachusetts, held a special event at their local mall during the holiday season. Shoppers who purchased a $10 ticket to the "Evening of Giving" got to attend a private after-hours shopping spree that featured holiday festivities, special sales at participating stores and a chance to win door prizes. The mall was closed to the general public; shopping was reserved exclusively to ticket holders.

Animal Shelter, Inc. held this event in partnership with the Simon Youth Foundation. The shelter received $7 of every ticket sold and the remaining $3 of each ticket sale went to the foundation, which fosters educational and career development for at-risk youth.

By partnering, both organizations benefited from the fundraiser. And people who hate crowds got to do their shopping in peace.

Level of...
- Difficulty = 🐾 🐾 🐾
- Planning Time = 🕐 🕐 🕐 🕐
- Upfront Costs = 💰 💰 💰
- Personnel = 👤 👤 👤 👤

20

Sell Calendars of Adopted Pets

Every adopted pet has a story, so why not share these stories? People love happy endings and one way to get the word out about the success stories is to put them in a calendar. You can create calendars using a variety of computer software programs like Microsoft Publisher or more elaborate graphic design software. (If you are lucky enough to have a graphic artist among your supporters, enlist his or her help on the project.) Be sure to include photos of the happy critters in their new homes.

You can print the calendars yourself and have them wire-bound at an office supply store like Staples or you can work with an offset printer if you plan to create a lot of calendars. This option requires much more money up-front, so you'll need to make sure you set a budget for the project.

Level of...

- Difficulty = 🐾 🐾 🐾
- Planning Time = 🕐 🕐 🕐
- Upfront Costs = 💰 💰 💰 💰
- Personnel = 👤 👤

21

Have a Virtual Cat Walk

Many organizations do dog walks, but what about the cats? The SPCA of Central Florida found a creative solution to this problem. Instead of attempting to walk cats at a live event, the organization opted to do a "virtual cat walk" called the Meow March. They used the power of the Internet to recruit more than 100 cats and their humans for a virtual walk from Florida to Washington.

Each "walker" signed up online and could customize a fundraising Web page to solicit pledges from their friends and family. Even though the cats didn't leave the house, the event raised more than $14,000. Armed with only a bit of tech savvy, you can turn this type of virtual event into a moneymaker.

Level of...
- Difficulty = 🐾 🐾 🐾 🐾
- Planning Time = 🕐 🕐 🕐
- Upfront Costs = 💰 💰
- Personnel = 🧍 🧍 🧍

22

The Flamingo Fundraiser

A popular fundraiser is to use something really ugly and get people to pay to have it removed from their yard. Often referred to as the "Flamingo Fundraiser," it traditionally involves placing a large group of pink flamingos in someone's yard. The owner has to pay a donation to have the pink birds relocated. Alternate versions of this idea include placing items like ugly gnomes or other questionable yard art. The main thing is for the item to be funny and very visible.

Another twist is that the person who asks to have flamingos removed from his yard also gets the opportunity to choose the next yard art "victim." The yard art is generally funny in some way, so you are likely to garner a lot of great human-interest stories from the local press.

Of course, you will have to create flyers to explain the fundraiser, because you do need to make sure the participants know about it and think the idea is funny!

Level of...
- Difficulty = 🐾 🐾
- Planning Time = 🕐 🕐 🕐
- Upfront Costs = 💰 💰 💰
- Personnel = 👤 👤

23

Hawgs for Dawgs

Avid motorcyclists look for any excuse to ride, so use this to your advantage. For example, the White River Humane Society in Indiana benefited from a 115-mile road trip called "Hawgs for Dawgs." Organizers expected 50-100 participants for the ride, which was a "poker run" type of ride. At various stops along the trip, riders have to draw a card. The rider with the best poker hand at the end of the ride wins a prize. The group also awarded prizes for the worst poker hand, oldest rider, the youngest rider, and the longest distance traveled.

A similar event in Colorado that was run in conjunction with Harley-Davidson dealers attracted 300 riders who raised more than $11,000 in pledges for Best Friends Animal Society.

Level of...
- Difficulty = 🐾 🐾
- Planning Time = 🕐 🕐 🕐
- Upfront Costs = 💰 💰
- Personnel = 🧍 🧍

24

Sell a Pet Treat Cookbook

Church groups and other religious organizations have been selling cookbooks as fundraisers for years, so why shouldn't you? To make it relevant to pet owners, consider collecting recipes for pet treats instead of recipes for human consumption. The most-labor intensive part is collecting enough recipes to fill an entire cookbook.

Publishing companies exist that specialize in cookbooks used as fundraisers. If you go this route, you just send them the recipes and they lay out the book and print it for you. (Of course you will have some up-front costs for this, so make sure to budget for it!)

Alternatively, you can lay it out yourself and have it copied and bound in small quantities at a quick-print shop or office supply store like Staples.

Once the cookbook is complete, you can sell it to everyone who contributed and at various locations in your community. A shelter in Canada included a complete "treat mix" and cookie cutter with its cookbook. Of course, the package included lots of information about how the purchase benefited the animals!

Level of...

- Difficulty = 🐾 🐾 🐾 🐾
- Planning Time = 🕐 🕐 🕐 🕐
- Upfront Costs = 💰 💰 💰 💰 💰
- Personnel = 👤 👤 👤

25

Cans for Cats

In Sioux City, Iowa, the Community Theatre decided to turn a show into a fundraiser for the Humane Society. They developed a clever "Cans for Cats" promotion associated with their production of Tennessee Williams' play "Cat on a Hot Tin Roof."

Instead of requiring people to purchase a ticket, the cast opted to use a "can" as the price of admission. The "can" could be a can of pet food, a monetary donation or any other item that would benefit a four-legged resident of the humane society, such as cleaning supplies, paper and cloth towels, and dog and cat toys.

In the words of Mickey Rooney, "Let's put on a show!"

Level of...
- Difficulty = 🐾 🐾 🐾 🐾
- Planning Time = 🕐 🕐 🕐 🕐
- Upfront Costs = 💰 💰 💰 💰
- Personnel = 🧍 🧍 🧍 🧍 🧍

26

Holiday Gift Wrapping

During the holidays people are extremely busy. Many stores don't offer gift-wrapping services, so capitalize on that and ask a local mall or store if you can set up a gift-wrapping stand. People pay you to wrap their gifts while they are shopping.

All you need is wrapping paper, boxes, tape, scissors and willing volunteers. Find sources willing to donate wrapping paper and boxes. (You'd be surprised what people have lying around the house!) During the event, don't forget to put up signs to let people know that the wrapping service is a gift they can give to the animals and that extra donations are gladly accepted.

Level of...

- Difficulty = 🐾 🐾
- Planning Time = 🕐 🕐 🕐
- Upfront Costs = 💰 💰
- Personnel = 🧍 🧍

27

Pet Photo Contest

A photo contest is a fairly easy way to raise funds. For example, the Greater Huntsville Humane Society sponsors an annual "Hot Dogs and Cool Cats" photo contest for their calendar. They ask cat and dog owners to submit photos of their favorite pets. Entrants pay a fee to submit their photo, and the public pays $1 each to vote for their favorite photos, which are included in a calendar. The photos are displayed and people can vote as many times as they want, either by mail or in person. The humane society raised more than $57,000 with this fundraiser.

As an alternative, if you don't have a good way to offer public voting, you might enlist a professional photographer, magazine editor, and other local media celebrities to act as judges. In this case, you can offer great (donated) prizes for the winners.

Level of...
- Difficulty = 🐾 🐾 🐾
- Planning Time = 🕐 🕐 🕐
- Upfront Costs = 💰 💰
- Personnel = 👤 👤

28

Sell a House

It's not unheard of for people to donate houses to non-profit organizations. Recently, in Arkansas City, Kansas, the Cowley County Humane Society closed a deal on a donated house for more than $60,000. The proceeds are being used for improving the shelter facility and to endow a new foundation upon which future donations can build.

It's also possible to raffle a house. College or high school carpentry programs sometimes build houses and then raffle them off. Ticket prices have to be quite high, but the payoff is huge for the winner! If you have construction labor at your disposal, you might use a twist on this idea by fixing up houses that need TLC and reselling them at a profit.

Level of...

- Difficulty = 🐾 🐾 🐾 🐾 🐾
- Planning Time = 🕐 🕐 🕐
- Upfront Costs = 💰 💰 💰 💰 💰
- Personnel = 🧍 🧍 🧍 🧍 🧍

29

Event Poster Contest and Raffle/Auction

If you have a big fundraising event every year, odds are good that you will create promotional posters to display around your community. Make those posters do double duty by making the posters a fundraiser themselves. First run a poster design contest to select an artist, then later raffle or auction off the original artwork, and sell the posters. Each part of the process is a public relations opportunity for your organization.

Because you are getting artists to design the poster, odds are good the winning poster will be really eye-catching and colorful. In some areas, people collect posters for annual events because the artwork is so beautiful. When that happens, you can bring out signed collector's editions of your posters too!

Level of...
- Difficulty = 🐾 🐾 🐾
- Planning Time = 🕐 🕐 🕐
- Upfront Costs = 💰 💰
- Personnel = 🧍 🧍 🧍

30

Host a Yappy Hour

If your community has outdoor cafes or bars and restaurants with outdoor seating areas, consider hosting "Yappy Hours." The Doña Ana County Humane Society in Las Cruces, New Mexico, holds these monthly "interspecies interactions" from April through October.

The humane society says that the regular events not only are an effective fundraiser, they also are a "friendraiser" that gives them an opportunity to inform people about the programs and activities of the organization. People pay a $6 donation to attend. The events typically draw about 70 people and their (leashed and vaccinated) pets.

Level of...

- Difficulty = 🐾 🐾 🐾
- Planning Time = 🕐 🕐 🕐 🕐
- Upfront Costs = 💰 💰
- Personnel = 🚹 🚹 🚹

31

Enlist a Car Dealership

In Iowa, a power promoter at the local car dealership helped organize a fundraiser for the Dubuque Humane Society. For one month the car dealership asks customers to bring in a bag of dog food. If a customer buys a car, $100 of the purchase price is donated to the humane society.

The humane society works with their local feed store to set up a dog food display in the car dealership showroom. In addition to the donations of dog food from the people buying cars and money from the dealership, because of the display people also donated gift certificates to the feed store. The gift certificates made it possible for the humane society to get supplies they needed in addition to the donated dog food.

The promotion is advertised on the radio and has netted the group more than $10,000 without very much effort, thanks to enthusiasm from the folks at the dealership.

Level of...
- Difficulty = 🐾 🐾 🐾
- Planning Time = 🕐 🕐 🕐
- Upfront Costs = 💰 💰
- Personnel = 👤 👤

32

Collect Small Change

Small change can really add up. An easy way to get small change is to place donation cans in shops around your town. Create donation cans using tin cans that come with a plastic lid, so you can cut a slit in the top. Customers can drop in coins after they make a purchase at the shop. If you want to get creative, enlist help from a local woodworker to make little wooden "dog houses" with a slit in a roof.

Make sure you put a label on the can or house that makes it very obvious where the money is going. Cute pictures of dogs and cats catch people's attention, so the better your photos or graphics, the more customers are likely to notice.

Someone will need to be in charge of picking up the donations on a regular basis (monthly or weekly) so the cans don't fill up and cause a problem for the merchants. You also will want to make sure that the can is in an area where someone can keep an eye on it, so it won't be stolen.

Another way to collect small change is to talk to the people in charge of the fountains in your community. Even when there are signs telling people not to throw change into fountains, some people feel compelled to do so. Take advantage of this fact by approaching the owner of the fountain and telling them you'll clean out the coins if you can keep them for your organization.

Level of...

- Difficulty = 🐾 🐾
- Planning Time = 🕐 🕐
- Upfront Costs = 💰 💰
- Personnel = 🧍 🧍

33

Sell Products on eBay

One way to make money, particularly if you run a thrift store is to sell items on eBay. For example, the Humane Society of Pagosa Springs in Colorado receives many donations to their thrift store. Some of the items are worth more than they could be sold for at the store, so since 1999, those pieces are placed on eBay. The eBay sales have turned into a nice monthly income for the organization.

Dog breed rescues also often sell craft items that have images of their favorite canines on them. When dog fanciers search on the breed name in eBay, the rescue's items come up. Because eBay is like the world's biggest yard sale, you don't even have to have any type of theme. Tell all your volunteers to look around their houses and see what items they were thinking of getting rid of and ask that they let you sell them on eBay instead.

Level of...
- Difficulty = 🐾 🐾 🐾
- Planning Time = 🕐 🕐
- Upfront Costs = 💰
- Personnel = 👤

34

Host a Telethon

Telethons aren't just for Jerry Lewis; some humane organizations have used telethons to raise money, too. For example, the Denver Dumb Friends League aired its first telethon in 1982. Their 2007 event raised a total of $212,000. During the telethon people hear real stories about the pets, see a tour the shelter, and learn about the DDFL services that help pets and people. The telethon features hosts from local TV and radio stations and local VIPs answer the phones.

Obviously a telethon is a huge event that requires a lot of planning, coordination and up-front money. However, if you can manage it, the payoff can be large.

Level of...

- Difficulty = 🐾 🐾 🐾 🐾 🐾
- Planning Time = 🕐 🕐 🕐 🕐 🕐
- Upfront Costs = 💰 💰 💰 💰
- Personnel = 👤 👤 👤 👤 👤

35

Have a Dog Walk

The traditional dog walk is one of the most popular fundraisers for pet-related organizations. This type of event can work in both large or small communities. The Maui Humane Society in Hawaii received $1,037 in pledges for their Bark in the Park event from just one seven-year-old girl. The event drew about 300 pet owners with 200 pets.

A smaller event in Stockton, California, called the Walk for the Animals, drew about 100 animals and 250 people who embarked on a one-mile pledge walk that was expected to raise about $28,000 to help run the Delta Humane Society and SPCA.

On a much larger scale, the 2007 14th annual "Furry Scurry" for the Denver Dumb Friend's League had 5,100 participants and brought in $826,000. When an event becomes popular, it can take on a life of its own and be something people really look forward to every year.

The Quincy Humane Society in Illinois has seen its "Mutt Strutt" fundraiser balloon from a few vendors and a few dozen dogs to more than 500 attendees and 200 animals. Earning $33,000 in 2009, the event has doubled its income in three years.

If you are thinking that a dog walk is too conventional or "old hat," think again. It's a perennial idea that still works year after year. After all, people love to get out and walk with their dogs!

Level of...

- Difficulty = 🐾 🐾 🐾
- Planning Time = 🕐 🕐 🕐 🕐
- Upfront Costs = 💰 💰 💰
- Personnel = 🧍 🧍 🧍 🧍

36

Eat for Pete

If you live in a town with a lot of restaurants, consider borrowing this cool idea from the Bradford County Humane Society in Ulster, Pennsylvania.

The shelter's most successful fundraiser is its "Eat for Pete" event that it does with local restaurants. Every year the Humane Society selects a dog and names him Pete. They photograph Pete and put him on posters around town encouraging people to eat out at participating restaurants on a particular evening. The slogan says that patrons can "Eat for Pete and all the other animals at the shelter so they know where their next meal is coming from." That night a portion of the restaurant's proceeds are donated to the shelter. The shelter also puts donation jars in the restaurants and information cards on the tables, describing their programs.

A related fundraiser in Bradford County is the "Shop for Pete" fundraiser, which uses the same concept with retailers. In both cases, the businesses and the shelter get a lot of publicity and of course, after being "spokes-dog," Pete gets a new home.

Level of...
- Difficulty = 🐾 🐾 🐾
- Planning Time = 🕐 🕐 🕐 🕐
- Upfront Costs = 💰 💰 💰
- Personnel = 👤 👤 👤

37

Gift Baskets or Boxes

Gift baskets are one of those things that you often can sell for more than you might expect. If your group already has a thrift store, by putting your items in a gift basket with pretty wrapping, you often can sell the package for more than you could the individual items.

Of course, you also can create baskets that have a pet theme. Include collars, IDs, and other items that promote responsible pet ownership. If you add more high-end goodies like gift certificates from vet clinics, you can auction off the baskets.

You can use other containers in addition to baskets. Sometimes baskets are extremely inexpensive at thrift stores, but so are mugs and pretty bowls. Anything that can hold a bunch of goodies and be tied up with a bow can work as a "basket," so be creative!

Level of...
- Difficulty = 🐾 🐾
- Planning Time = 🕐 🕐
- Upfront Costs = 💰 💰 💰
- Personnel = 🧍 🧍

38

Horse Show

Although it's not a typical fundraiser for an animal shelter, the Berkshire Humane Society in Massachusetts holds a horse show every summer. The show is recognized by the Western Massachusetts Professional Horseman's Association and since its inception has raised more than $120,000 for the Berkshire Humane Society, which helps about 2,000 animals each year.

The horse show is held at Overmeade Farm in Lenox and includes competitions for all levels of riding with hunter, equitation, and jumper divisions. The owners of the farm have held the fundraiser for years and the best part is that all the money goes to help the animals.

Level of...

- Difficulty = 🐾 🐾 🐾 🐾
- Planning Time = 🕐 🕐 🕐 🕐
- Upfront Costs = 💰 💰 💰 💰
- Personnel = 👤 👤 👤 👤 👤

39

Don't Come Fundraiser

One of the easiest fundraisers to do is the classic "don't come" event. With this type of fundraiser, you make up an event and then tell people not to show up. The cost is really low because you don't have to actually hold the event; your costs are just for mailing the invitations. Part of the fun is that you can invent the most outlandish, expensive event that no one will ever attend. Then mail invitations to all the busy people you can think of, such as your supporters, the media, and anyone else who appreciates a little humor.

For example, during one summer the Bakersfield SPCA sent out invitations asking donors to pay $100 not to cook hot dogs, $75 to avoid the softball game, $50 to stay out of traffic, $25 to avoid the bugs. Donors could enter any amount to avoid their "choice of irritant." The invitation billed it as the "greatest party you've never attended."

The party can be anything from a Christmas party to a sporting event. The more creative and funny, the better it works and the more likely you are to get a little free press, too.

Level of...
- Difficulty = 🐾
- Planning Time = 🕐 🕐
- Upfront Costs = 💰 💰 💰
- Personnel = 🧍

40

Adoption Stories Book

Over time, as you adopt out more and more critters, you'll undoubtedly accumulate a number of "happy ending" stories. After you have a good collection, you might end up with enough material for a book you can sell.

That's what the Coulee Region Humane Society in Wisconsin did with a book called *Tails from the Heart*. Filled with great stories of adopted pets, the book raised $18,000 for the Humane Society. The book was produced by volunteers, university students and community members who compiled 50 letters written by owners of animals that were adopted from the shelter. About 1,000 copies of the book were printed and were sold through the shelter.

Level of...

- Difficulty = 🐾 🐾 🐾 🐾 🐾
- Planning Time = 🕐 🕐 🕐 🕐
- Upfront Costs = 💰 💰 💰 💰
- Personnel = 🧍 🧍 🧍

41

Dog Wash

A dog wash can be a fun fundraiser. People have dogs and dogs get dirty, so get out there, clean them up, and raise some money. You'll need to get permission to use a park or area that has hot and cold running water available outside, where you can get to it. Or you might partner with a "dog wash facility" or groomer where bathtubs and water are available.

For example, the Dellaria Salons Paw Wash in Massachusetts helped raise money for MSPCA's Boston Animal Care and Adoption Center. The dog washes were held in the parking lot and cost $10. All proceeds were donated to the center. LaundroMutt, a self-service dog wash and dog spa, provided dog-friendly shampoo, scrubbers, brushes, and special drying towels. The local fire department provided fire hoses and the water supply.

Once you have enlisted partners and set up a place for the event, promote it everywhere. You'll draw more people if you have food for dog owners to eat while they wait for Fido to get clean. Also be sure to tell people that dogs being bathed must be on a leash and up to date on vaccinations.

Level of...
- Difficulty = 🐾 🐾 🐾
- Planning Time = 🕐 🕐 🕐
- Upfront Costs = 💰 💰 💰
- Personnel = 👤 👤 👤

42

Puppy Lottery or Bingo

If you've worked with puppies, you know that when they gotta go, they gotta go! You can take advantage of that and the fact that puppies are adorable, by setting up "lottery." People win when puppies make a deposit in a certain place.

This fundraiser is a variation of the "moo doo" lottery that is done with cows. If you are running an adopt-a-thon and have puppies out for people to see anyway, get an old Twister board and write numbers on the Twister dots. Then place it underneath an X pen with puppies in it. Inevitably puppies will do their thing.

Sell chances for $5-$10 a dot. Your lottery prize can be a donated gift. A related fundraiser is Puppy Bingo. In this case you mark off the area of ground where the puppies are with a grid. Have a Bingo tote board set up and sell Bingo cards.

The best thing is that during the lottery or bingo game people will get a chance to see the puppies and the pups are likely to be adopted. So bring their paperwork!

Level of...

- Difficulty = 🐾 🐾
- Planning Time = 🕐 🕐
- Upfront Costs = 💰 💰
- Personnel = 👤 👤 👤

43

Dog Fashion Show

Partner with clothing stores in your community to hold a fashion show. It's fun if you can get local celebrities to model the clothes, but volunteers or high school students make great models, too. Each model walks a dog down the runway. It's a fun way to show off your dogs and a great PR opportunity for the stores as well.

Sell tickets to the event and be sure to provide refreshments. You could tie it into a holiday like Valentine's Day or hold it near prom season, if your partner stores rent tuxes, for example. You supply the dogs; they supply the clothes. If you can, get a local radio personality to act as emcee for the event.

Level of...
- Difficulty = 🐾 🐾 🐾
- Planning Time = 🕐 🕐 🕐
- Upfront Costs = 💰 💰 💰
- Personnel = 👤 👤 👤 👤

44

Puppy/Kitten Shower

Every year puppy and kitten season rolls around. But instead of lamenting the inevitable, find a way to celebrate all those newborns. When humans are expecting a baby, people throw them a shower. So there's no reason not to throw your puppies and kittens a shower too.

Mail a letter or invitation saying that you are throwing a shower and create a list of all the supplies you'll need for the new arrivals. You'll want food, crates, toys, kitty litter, beds, and other "baby critter" items.

You can mail your invitations to your favorite donors and to stores that sell the supplies. You might want to make posters for the retail establishments, encouraging people to buy an extra item for the puppy or kitten shower.

You can turn the shower into an actual event to help draw people to your location and see all the new arrivals. Or you can make it simply a request for donations. Either way, do send out thank-you notes to all the people who participate in your shower, either in person or by making a donation.

Be sure to take a few pictures of the puppies and kittens, too. People love cute pictures and tend to pass them around, so some of your new arrivals might just get adopted!

Level of...

- Difficulty = 🐾 🐾
- Planning Time = 🕐 🕐
- Upfront Costs = 💰 💰
- Personnel = 👤

45

Dog Contests

If you are running a fundraising event, consider adding dog contests into the mix. For example, during its annual Bark in the Park fundraiser, the Natchez-Adams County Humane Society held a number of contests, such as cutest puppy, best costume, most friendly, most talented, most handsome male, most beautiful female, best mutt, and Mr. and Miss NACHS, titles given to dogs adopted from the shelter.

At the Bow Wow Pow Wow a few years ago, an Idaho shelter had fun contests that included Longest Tail, Best Begging Face, Miss Manners, and Dog/Owner Look-Alike. Local canine behaviorists and trainers acted as the judges. (I still have the ribbon my dog Leia won proudly displayed on my office wall!)

Every contest has an entry fee, so if you get a big turnout at your event, your contest can add quite a bit to the bottom line without too much extra effort.

Level of...
- Difficulty = 🐾 🐾 🐾
- Planning Time = 🕐 🕐 🕐
- Upfront Costs = 💰 💰
- Personnel = 🧍 🧍

46

Grocery Fundraisers

One way to make money is to involve your local grocery store. For a grocery coupon campaign, first you get volunteers to collect coupons from every place they can find. Then volunteers go into the grocery store and tape the appropriate coupons onto the products. Place cans at the register asking customers to "Give us a hand, drop your coupons in the can!"

Although it may seem like that little 25-cent coupon for kitty litter doesn't make much difference, the coupons add up quickly. At the end of the coupon drive, you tally up the coupons that have been donated and receive the redemption value from the grocery store. You do have to make sure that someone stops by to empty the cans (to make room for more coupons).

In Green Bay, Wisconsin, the Bay Area Humane Society ran a similar grocery store fundraiser. In this case, when shoppers purchased specially marked $5 or $10 bags of pet food and supplies, the items were donated to the Bay Area Humane Society.

The best part about working with a grocery store to raise money is that everyone has to eat!

Level of...
- Difficulty = 🐾 🐾
- Planning Time = 🕐 🕐
- Upfront Costs = 💰
- Personnel = 👤

47

Holiday Pet Photos

Many humane organizations do some type of "pet photos" fundraiser during the holiday season. In Washington, some people have been participating in the "Posing Pets & People with Santa" event for so many years that it has turned into a tradition. The fundraiser benefits the Kitsap Humane Society and is held at various locations in late November and throughout the month of December.

The Humane Society partners with a local photography studio and sells packages that range from $20 to $45. The photos (except for Christmas cards) are ready to take home the same day and all the proceeds go to the Humane Society. People bring small animals to locations such as pet stores and a local mall. The event located at the Kitsap Humane Society Barn even welcomes large animals like llamas and horses. Organizers say they'll take pictures of virtually any critter and even photos with no critters at all, if that's what people prefer.

Of course, when you do a "photos with Santa" type of event, you need someone to play Santa and you need a photographer. Hang up flyers everywhere and contact the media to get maximum exposure. Holiday Pet Photos are a great way to give people a smile during the holiday season and add a jingle to your pocket along the way.

Level of...

- Difficulty = 🐾 🐾
- Planning Time = 🕐 🕐 🕐
- Upfront Costs = 💰 💰
- Personnel = 🧍 🧍

48

Gala Event or Fur Ball

A really fancy "gala" event or "Fur Ball" can be a successful fundraiser, particularly if you can find corporate donors. In January, the Camden County Humane Society in Florida has its Denim & Diamonds Gala. Tickets cost $50; at the event, individual and corporate donors of $250 or more are recognized as "Humane Elite" sponsors. Sponsorship also includes a free ticket to the gourmet buffet dinner, a live auction and dance. According to a news story, guests for the event are encouraged to "dress creatively in blue jeans bottoms and fancy tops."

This type of event requires a lot of up-front planning. You should have it at a really fancy venue and ask people to dress up in their best finery. If you have a millionaire supporter, a museum, or an historic house in your town, ask if the event could be hosted at that location. Many people will attend, just to have the opportunity to see areas of the venue that are usually off-limits to the general public. Any way you can make the event more "elite," exclusive or special in some way will increase the number of attendees.

Level of...

- Difficulty = 🐾 🐾 🐾 🐾
- Planning Time = 🕐 🕐 🕐 🕐
- Upfront Costs = 💰 💰 💰 💰
- Personnel = 🧍 🧍 🧍 🧍

49

Partner with a Business

Any time a business owner expresses support for your organization, try to capitalize on that. Partnering with a business on a fundraiser benefits both you and the business. For example, virtually every town has restaurants. That's just one type of business you can easily partner with to host an event. The type of restaurant doesn't matter.

For example, in Baltimore, Clarence's Taste of New Orleans held a charity event to benefit the Humane Society of Harford County. And in Utica, New York, the Uno Chicago Grill had a "Dough Raiser" for the Stevens-Swan Humane Society. The bottom line is that people like to go out to eat.

Any time someone who owns a business says, "I'd like to help the animals," take the time to think of ways a partnership can be a "win-win" for both of you. Every business wants more good publicity and customers. You want more funds to care for animals. It can be a match made in business heaven and if all goes well, the partnership can last for years.

Level of...

- Difficulty = 🐾 🐾 🐾
- Planning Time = 🕐 🕐 🕐
- Upfront Costs = 💰 💰 💰
- Personnel = 👤 👤 👤 👤

50

Groom-a-rama

Groomers are almost invariably dog-lovers, so recruit them for a "groom-a-thon" fundraiser. With this fundraiser, generally the groomers keep their tips, but the humane organization receives the grooming fees as a donation.

For example, Pet Love, a mobile pet-grooming service in the Dallas-Fort Worth area, got great results from its "Don't Forget the Animals" one-day pet groom-a-thon, which benefited pets injured or displaced by Hurricane Katrina.

The minimum donation was $25, but many people donated $75 or $100 per pet. People also dropped off items like food, collars, and crates. Some people even drove by and just handed the groomers cash. All of the net proceeds from the event were shared by the Society for the Prevention of Cruelty to Animals of Texas in Dallas (SPCA) and the Humane Society of North Texas in Fort Worth (HSNT) to support their efforts to care for animals who were victims of the hurricane.

Level of...

- Difficulty = 🐾 🐾 🐾
- Planning Time = 🕐 🕐 🕐
- Upfront Costs = 💰 💰
- Personnel = 👤 👤 👤 👤

51

Pet Sitting

A variation of the "rent-a-kid" for a day fundraiser is to have a "pet sitter for a day." You just need to recruit volunteers who are willing to go into homes and feed and walk the dog or play with the cats and clean the kitty litter.

Entice donors with the idea of just taking an afternoon off from all their pet responsibilities. Call it the "Dog Day Afternoon" fundraiser. The pet-sitting fees benefit the humane organization. Like any good pet sitter or dog walker, volunteers should leave little notes for the owners, so they know their pets were in good hands. And of course, it's a great opportunity to say thank you and leave behind your newsletter too, so people know how their donation will be used.

Level of...

- Difficulty = 🐾 🐾
- Planning Time = 🕐 🕐 🕐
- Upfront Costs = 💰
- Personnel = 🧍 🧍 🧍

52

Promote Planned Giving

Planned giving is asking donors to make a contribution to your organization either now or in the future through a will, endowment, insurance or investment beneficiary designation, or a gift of property.

The main thing about planned giving is to let prospective donors know that it's an option. Estate planning is something that people don't think about often, but when they do, you want them to know that you'd appreciate being included in their plans. Add a page to your Web site or put a notice in your newsletter to remind people to talk to their lawyer when they draw up a will. People often give either a percentage of their estate or a specific dollar amount. If you have multiple programs, let people know that if they wish, they can limit their donation to just that program, such as a spay/neuter program or a building fund. Work with your lawyer to make sure the verbiage on your planned giving suggestions is both workable and legal.

Memorial gifts are another option for those who want to honor a deceased family member or friend. A related gift is a pet memorial gift to honor the memory of a beloved pet. Point out that planned giving also can result in a tax deduction, assuming your organization is a 501(c)(3) non-profit.

It's a good idea to include planned giving in your fundraising mix. The Denver Dumb Friends League 2007 annual report shows that the organization received "$1,633,166 from the estates of 42 people."

Level of...

- Difficulty = 🐾 🐾
- Planning Time = 🕐 🕐 🕐
- Upfront Costs = 💰
- Personnel = 👤

53

Dachshund Race

Consider having a race that showcases a particular breed of dog. This type of event can be particularly amusing if the breed of dog is one that people normally don't associate with being speedy. For example, the Tri-Lakes Humane Society in Missouri holds a "Dachshund Dash" in the summer. Entrants pay a fee and the humane society encourages donations as well. The rules state that the dog "must be a certified Weiner dog - This does not mean they have to be AKC registered. If their shot record from the vet indicates the breed of dog is a dachshund, then it is a wiener dog" ('nuff said).

People love watching all those "wiener dogs" go! Plus, funny dog races are great fodder for human-interest stories on the TV news, so your odds of getting coverage are high.

The dachshund race is yet another example of how you can incorporate humor into your events. It definitely puts the "fun" in fundraising.

Level of...

- Difficulty = 🐾 🐾
- Planning Time = 🕐 🕐 🕐
- Upfront Costs = 💰 💰 💰
- Personnel = 👤 👤 👤

54

Rent a Pet

In the last year or so, companies have come up with the idea of "renting a pet" for those who can't have one because of a busy schedule or their living situation. What is a business opportunity for those companies can easily be transformed into a fundraising opportunity for you.

Run a "rent a pet" fundraiser asking people to pay a fee to take a dog out for a walk or to play with a kitty. It's a great way to increase interest in your volunteer and foster programs and, at the same time, give your animals more opportunities for socialization.

You can set this up as a "rent a pet for an afternoon" event in conjunction with an open house or make it an opportunity for people to pay a specific amount to play pet owner for an entire month.

Level of...
- Difficulty = 🐾 🐾
- Planning Time = 🕐 🕐
- Upfront Costs = 💰
- Personnel = 🧍 🧍 🧍

55

Create a Pinup Calendar

A few years ago, a movie called "Calendar Girls" told the story of a group of English women who raised money by creating a "girly" pinup calendar with women (minus clothing) posed among strategically located props.

Humane groups can easily adapt this idea. In fact, the Animal League of Gaston County did just that with a calendar called Pearls and Paws: Bare Because We Care. The calendar featured a series of photographs of women lounging in their birthday suits behind carefully placed dogs and cats. The sepia-toned photos were accompanied by animal quotes and statistics.

According to an article about the fundraiser, producing the calendars was expensive, but assuming all 5,000 calendars were sold, the total amount raised for the animals was projected to be around $100,000.

Level of...

- Difficulty = 🐾 🐾 🐾
- Planning Time = 🕐 🕐 🕐
- Upfront Costs = 💰 💰 💰 💰 💰
- Personnel = 👤 👤 👤

56

Flea or Farmers' Market

A garage or yard sale is a great fundraiser, but if your community has a regular flea market or farmers' market, another way to make money is to exhibit there. Although you may have to pay for booth space, the cost will be offset by the fact that in most communities, markets are extremely well attended because the time and location don't change.

In many areas, flea/farmers' markets run for several hours every weekend. If you participate regularly and sell donated items, you can create a steady source of income. If you have a thrift store, bringing some of your best items to display at a neighborhood market can be a great way to move inventory by exposing it to an audience that may not visit your store. It's also an opportunity to educate people about what you do and encourage them to donate their unwanted items for you to sell at the next market. Of course, you'll also want to bring along a donation jar just in case people have some spare cash they'd like to donate!

Level of...

- Difficulty = 🐾 🐾
- Planning Time = 🕐 🕐 🕐
- Upfront Costs = 💰 💰
- Personnel = 👤 👤 👤

57

Pet Talent Show

David Letterman isn't the only one with pet tricks. A talent (or even a no-talent) show is a great way to raise money. You can include the show as part of a larger pet fundraiser or have a stand-alone show. You can include pets or not. For example, you might put on a vaudeville-type show that has a pet theme but no actual pets on stage.

A number of humane groups around the country have a "WestMUTTster" Dog Show, which sometimes includes entertainment and demonstrations. In South Carolina, the WestMUTTster show put on by the Aiken Society for the Prevention of Cruelty to Animals draws about 500 people and includes working-dog demonstrations by the Aiken Department of Public Safety, the Palmetto Dog Club, the Aiken Bloodhound Team and the Aiken County Sheriff's Office.

In New York City, skateboarding, carriage-pushing and piano playing dogs were the entertainment at the "Charm School & Talent Show," judged by a panel of celebrity judges, including Tony award-winner Bernadette Peters.

Level of...

- Difficulty = 🐾 🐾 🐾
- Planning Time = 🕐 🕐 🕐 🕐
- Upfront Costs = 💰 💰 💰 💰
- Personnel = 🧍 🧍 🧍 🧍

58

Sponsor a Kennel

When you set up a cage or kennel sponsorship program, you give corporations or individuals the opportunity to directly help in the care of the animals.

The Animal Welfare Society of Maine has been offering kennel sponsorship for years. They ask for pledges to sponsor a cage or kennel for "as little as $20 a month for a dog (that's 67 cents a day) or $10 a month for a cat (that's 33 cents a day)." As they point out in their promotion, just a few cents per day helps keep the animals "happy, well fed and warm and dry until they join their new families."

The AWS distributes flyers about the program and invites people to sign up for sponsorship online at their Web site as well. People just fill out the online form and mail it in. A plaque recognizing each sponsor is attached to a cage or kennel at the shelter. Each kennel can have up to four sponsors, which amounts to $960 for each dog kennel and $480 for each cat cage. Your only expenses are the cost of having plaques made and the cost of printing flyers if you choose to promote sponsorship by distributing flyers.

Level of...
- Difficulty = 🐾 🐾
- Planning Time = 🕐 🕐
- Upfront Costs = 💰 💰
- Personnel = 🧍

59

Online Donation Sites

Registering as a charity at online donation sites like iGive.com, MyCause.com, and Heartof.com are a great way to add a few dollars to your coffers. Using iGive, people shop online at more than 680 stores; a portion of each purchase is donated to their favorite charity. People find their favorite charity in the list and then join the site. At this point about 25,000 charities are in the list; there's no reason you can't be one of them.

Once you are registered at the charitable sites, be sure to let people know about it in all your promotional materials. In your newsletter, tell your members to be sure to do all their online shopping through these sites. It may seem like a small thing, but all those online shopping dollars can really add up, with minimal effort on your part. After you sign up, all you have to do is deposit the checks.

Level of...

- Difficulty = 🐾
- Planning Time = 🕐
- Upfront Costs = 🕐
- Personnel = 🧍

60

Comedy Night

Most people can use a good laugh, so take advantage of that by hosting a comedy night. In Riverside County, California, the Riverside Humane Society Pet Adoption Center has held an annual Comedy Night for many years. The most recent event featured comedian and actor Henry Cho; it surpassed previous years in attendance and money earned. Proceeds from sponsorships, admission tickets, silent and live auctions and raffle-ticket sales totaled $43,000, a gain of $9,000 over the previous year. The event drew 285 people (a 30 percent increase) and boasted more sponsors and higher raffle-ticket sales.

If course, the real key to having a comedy night fundraiser is finding a great comedian. Your first step is to consider the old "six degrees of separation" concept. Among your board members, donors, fans, adopters and friends, someone may know someone who knows a comedian who might be willing to perform for a good cause. Failing that approach, scout around for local or regional talent. The worst response will be "no," but if the response is "yes," you can start laughing all the way to the bank.

Level of...

- Difficulty = 🐾 🐾 🐾
- Planning Time = 🕐 🕐 🕐 🕐
- Upfront Costs = 💰 💰 💰
- Personnel = 🧍 🧍 🧍

61

Ask for Beds and Get Food

The Kuranda "chew proof" dog bed Web site has a "Donate-a-Bed" program, allowing individuals to donate beds to the shelter of their choice at discounted prices (http://kuranda.com). The beds are hammock-style and are made of PVC frames and heavy-duty vinyl fabrics. Because they are easy to clean and disinfect, they are great for shelters and rescues.

You need to contact the company to have your humane group listed on the site, but it can reap great rewards, particularly if you promote the fact that you'd like the beds. During the holiday season, the Elmsford Humane Society in New York received 202 donated beds.

Certain pet food companies donate food. Hills Pet Food (http://www.hillspet.com) offers the Science Diet Shelter Nutrition Partnership. If you sign up, you receive enough Science Diet brand pet food to feed *all* of the animals in your care. You pay for shipping and handling, but the food is delivered to your door.

You also can get sample bags of food to give out with every adoption. A testimonial from the Humane Society of Willamette Valley in Oregon says they saved $5,000 in food costs by participating.

Getting products like food and beds at no cost means you can put the money you would have spent into other programs!

Level of...

- Difficulty = 🐾
- Planning Time = 🕐
- Upfront Costs = 💰
- Personnel = 👤

62

Raffle Items from Crafters and Artisans

If you live in an arts community, ask artisans and crafters to donate items for you to raffle. Quilt guilds often will create beautiful handmade quilts for charity, so put your organization on their list. You may have to wait months or years for your quilt, but it is invariably worth the wait!

If you have a volunteer who is a crafter, you can ask if he or she is willing to donate items for a raffle. The Clark County Humane Society in Wisconsin held a "Cats Rule" raffle during the summer. The humane society raffled off a number of beautiful quilted items created by one of its volunteers. The quilt, sweatshirt, wall hanging, tote bags and potholders were created especially for the raffle and donated to the humane society. All of the items featured kitty themes and used feline-oriented fabrics.

Level of...
- Difficulty = 🐾 🐾
- Planning Time = 🕐 🕐
- Upfront Costs = 💰
- Personnel = 👤

63

Have a Combo Fundraiser

Setting up a fundraising event can be a lot of work. One way to get more "bang for your buck" is to run a "combo" fundraiser with a number of events that all occur on the same day. Rounding up a willing cadre of volunteers multiple times a year can be challenging for some organizations. By running several events at once, you can get everyone really fired up for one serious fundraising push and save on promotional costs, too.

On one Saturday in September, the White River Humane Society in Indiana held a Walk, Ride, and Rocks fundraiser. They combined two previously separate fundraisers: the Mutt Strut and a motorcycle poker run. The dog walk was in the morning and the motorcycle event ran during the afternoon. The humane society added a third event that evening—a concert featuring music from five local bands. At the concert the WRHS Executive Director was able to announce the results from the dog walk and motorcycle poker run (both events were successful).

Planning three events for the same day is a lot of work, but in certain situations it makes sense; it's a day to remember. (Then everyone can spend the next week recovering!)

Level of...

- Difficulty = 🐾 🐾 🐾 🐾
- Planning Time = 🕐 🕐 🕐 🕐
- Upfront Costs = 💰 💰 💰
- Personnel = 👤 👤 👤 👤

64

Have a Tea Party

Tea parties aren't just for Alice (of Wonderland fame) or the British. You can turn the tradition of classic afternoon tea into a great fundraiser, too.

In Naples, Florida, guests of the Classic Afternoon Tea benefit toddled off to the Naples Hilton to sip tea and support the work of the humane society. The tea party was held in the traditional English style with a selection of blended teas, English tea sandwiches, and desserts. A number of sponsors contributed a variety of items for a silent auction, including season tickets to Florida Everblades hockey games and a $1,000 gift certificate for a jewelry store. More than 250 people purchased an $85 ticket for a seat at the event.

Level of...
- Difficulty = 🐾 🐾 🐾
- Planning Time = 🕐 🕐 🕐
- Upfront Costs = 💰 💰 💰
- Personnel = 👤 👤 👤

65

50-50 Raffle

A 50-50 raffle is a raffle in which the proceeds are split in half. Fifty percent of the money raised goes to the fundraising group, and fifty percent goes to the winner of the raffle. Let's face it, people like cash. It's the prize everyone wants to win.

The Chesapeake Humane Society sold $1 tickets for a 50-50 raffle and the winner won more than $2,000. That means that the CHS got $2,000 too. All from a bunch of $1 tickets. A 50-50 raffle is great for regular meetings too, because it makes a super-easy door prize. Just sell tickets as people walk in the door.

Level of...

- Difficulty = 🐾
- Planning Time = 🕐
- Upfront Costs = 💰
- Personnel = 🧍

66

Chocoholics Unite

Chocoholics are a passionate group. Give them what they want (more chocolate!) and they'll give you money in return. Of course, many groups sell chocolate bars as a fundraiser, but you can get quite a bit more creative. For the last two years the Humane Society of Somerset County, Pennsylvania, has held an event called "Coco's Extravaganza," which features chocolate fountains. Organizers said they had a "fantastic" response because people want to help the animals and they love chocolate.

Along with the chocolate fountains, the event featured desserts, champagne punch, door prizes, silent and oriental auctions, basket raffles and drawings. The first year the group sold 220 tickets, but they upped the number to tickets to 350, so the event is expected to raise more than $15,000. Volunteers were recruited from the local high school and guests were greeted by shelter dogs.

Chocolate is just as popular in Arkansas. In 2008, the Humane Society of Faulkner County brought out their own chocolate fountains for their 13th annual "Chocoholics Dream Night Out." The prior year's event broke records, proving that even after a decade, chocoholics apparently never get tired of their favorite food.

Level of...

- Difficulty = 🐾 🐾 🐾
- Planning Time = 🕐 🕐 🕐 🕐
- Upfront Costs = 💰 💰 💰
- Personnel = 👤 👤 👤

67

Chinese Auction

A Chinese auction is sort of a combination raffle and auction. The way it works is that people buy tickets for a set price. At the auction, each item being auctioned has a bowl or basket sitting in front of it. People write their name and phone number on one of their tickets and drop it into the basket in front of the item they want. People can put as many tickets as they want into any basket, so if someone really wants something, they'll drop in a whole bunch of tickets (which is what you want them to do). The more tickets you sell, the more money you'll make.

At the end of the auction period, a volunteer draws the winning ticket from the basket in front of each item. Popular items may have a basket jam-packed with tickets. You'll want to have ticket sellers working the room in case people run out of tickets and want to offer more bids. (Of course, you want to be right there ready to sell them more!)

Level of...

- Difficulty = 🐾 🐾 🐾
- Planning Time = 🕐 🕐 🕐 🕐
- Upfront Costs = 💰 💰 💰
- Personnel = 🧍 🧍 🧍

68

Set Up a Wish List

A wish list is an often-overlooked method of soliciting donations, possibly because it's so simple. Basically a wish list is a list of items that you always need for your organization, such as food, kitty litter, towels, stamps, and other items.

The key to creating a wish list is to make it very specific. If you feed only a particular brand of food or use a certain type of kitty litter, make sure you specify it. The Humane Society of Central Illinois explains exactly what they need for their office, animals and building.

Once you have set up a wish list, post it everywhere. Put it on your Web site, in your newsletter, and make flyers to hang up and share with people. You know what you need, so let people know!

Level of...

- Difficulty = 🐾 🐾
- Planning Time = 🕐 🕐
- Upfront Costs = 💰 💰
- Personnel = 🧍

69

License Plates

This idea involves getting involved with your state government, but if you have political animals in your midst, it's worth a try to get funding through special state license plates. In some areas, specialized license plates provide a tremendous amount of funding for non-profit groups.

For example, in Alabama a new spay-neuter license plate has been approved by the Alabama Department of Revenue. Like other specialized tags in the state, the spay-neuter tags cost $50. Out of that $50, $41.25 goes to the Alabama Veterinary Medical Foundation to assist low-income families with the cost of spaying and neutering their pets.

The Lee County Humane Society has been involved in the effort to get the plates produced. During this year-long campaign, at least 1,000 people in the state of Alabama must commit to purchasing the tag in order for the state to manufacture them. Although it may be a long, bureaucratic road, $41,000 can spay and neuter a lot of animals!

Level of...

- Difficulty = 🐾 🐾 🐾 🐾 🐾
- Planning Time = 🕐 🕐 🕐 🕐
- Upfront Costs = 💰 💰
- Personnel = 👤

70

Celebrity Connection

Take advantage of the fact that people are easily star-struck and include celebrities in your fundraising activities. Even small towns have local celebrities, such as radio and TV personalities, whom you can enlist to participate in dog walks or to emcee an event. The celebrity involvement doesn't have to be an in-person appearance, either.

In Nebraska, during the Beatrice Humane Society's annual "Paws-itively Desserts" fundraiser, the group auctioned off a number of items signed by or acquired from famous people.

One intrepid volunteer went to a Web site called www.ContactAnyCelebrity.com, where you can pay a fee to get the addresses of celebrities. She then mailed about 200 letters requesting donations from celebrities.

The results included an autographed CD and cap from George Strait; autographed photos from Richard Petty, Betty White, Greg Norman and Martina McBride; Thomas Kinkaid prints; an autographed copy of a Dean Koontz book; an autographed Nebraska Volleyball NCAA 2006-2007 champions poster; and an autographed Paula Dean cookbook. Even Elvira donated something to the auction.

Given that the event generally brings in between $20,000-$25,000 (about a quarter of the Beatrice Humane Society's budget), it was certainly worth it to write a few letters to famous people.

Level of...

- Difficulty = 🐾 🐾
- Planning Time = 🕐 🕐 🕐 🕐
- Upfront Costs = 💰 💰 💰
- Personnel = 👤 👤

71

Open a Thrift Store

If you want to take your fundraising to the next level and create a long-term source of funds, consider opening a thrift store. Starting and running a thrift store is complicated and not without risk, but it can pay off. Be sure to do your research by talking to other thrift stores and non-profits in your area, so you can choose a location and legal setup that works well. As with any business, you have to deal with hiring and training staff and volunteers; acquiring, sorting and displaying inventory; and accounting tasks. The demands are significant, but so are the results.

Initially, the board at the Crawford County Humane Society in Meadville, Pennsylvania, wasn't convinced that LeRoy Stearns's idea to start a thrift store would solve their financial woes. But Stearns put up $25,000 of his own money and set to work creating the Second Chance Thrift Store.

After researching areas and talking to other thrift store managers, he found a location, set up displays, and organized the staff and volunteers. The results were impressive. With its cheery, clean environment, the store has become a popular spot in town and turns a substantial profit.

Not only does the thrift store attract bargain hunters, it also continues to advertise the Humane Society's mission. Although they were dubious at first, the board couldn't be more thrilled with Stearns's results. After two years in business, the thrift store reportedly brought in about $400,000 in 2004. And $280,000 of it was profit that went directly to the Crawford County Humane Society.

Level of...

- Difficulty = 🐾 🐾 🐾 🐾 🐾
- Planning Time = 🕐 🕐 🕐 🕐 🕐
- Upfront Costs = 💰 💰 💰 💰 💰
- Personnel = 🐾 🐾 🐾 🐾 🐾

72

Cat Tree Kits

A cat tree kit is an easy and inexpensive product to make. Check the Internet and select a cat tree template that you like (and that cats enjoy). Then talk to Home Depot or your local hardware store to see if you can get donated or discounted plywood, lumber, nails, and tools.

Carpeting or furniture stores can be good resources for remnant carpet to cover the tree platforms. Enlist a few woodworking volunteers or a local high school shop class to cut the wood and pre-drill nail holes.

Make a variety of kits, so your customers can choose carpet colors to match their house. Once you have created the kits, bundle the parts together with string or put them in an attractive and easy-to-carry bag. Be sure to include clear assembly instructions as well.

If your woodworking volunteers get into the cat tree project, you might expand to other types of kits as well. Birdhouses, small scratching posts, dog houses, spice racks, and holiday ornaments are all simple projects for woodworkers. In addition to looking for skilled volunteer labor at high schools, you can check with local art and vocational schools. Just remember to keep the cost of the kits down, so you don't spend too much on your kit inventory.

Spend some time making signs and displays for your kits, so your patrons will be inspired to buy for your good cause!

Level of...

- Difficulty = 🐾 🐾 🐾
- Planning Time = 🕐 🕐 🕐
- Upfront Costs = 💰 💰
- Personnel = 🧍 🧍

73

Create Tiered Memberships

Many groups have just one level of membership: you pay $25 or $50 and you are a member of the organization. But you can increase your income if you add different membership levels.

For example, the Naperville Humane Society in Illinois offers five different membership levels, each offering different benefits. At the low end, Shelter "Friends" are honored with a plaque at the shelter, acknowledgement in the newsletter, shelter tours and discounts. At the top end, "Visionary Level" members receive all the benefits of the lower levels, plus perks like free seating at events, listing on event signage and a kennel plaque engraved with a message.

Think about the extra benefits you can offer to your most ardent supporters. What perks can you give them? With some creative offerings, you might just increase your membership and your income at the same time.

Level of...
- Difficulty = 🐾 🐾
- Planning Time = 🕐 🕐 🕐 🕐
- Upfront Costs = 💰 💰 💰
- Personnel = 🧍 🧍

74

Sell Greeting Cards

Everyone loves receiving cards, and selling greeting cards can be a simple way to raise money. For one thing, if you have a good photographer among your volunteers, you have a ready supply of adorable fuzzy models he or she can use for your card artwork.

Your card-selling options are quite varied. At the low end, you can take a do-it-yourself approach by making your cards using a color printer and fancy papers. Or you can opt for full four-color printing from online printing companies such as PrintingforLess.com, VistaPrint.com or even Shutterfly.com. If you choose an online printing company, you just upload your photos or designs and let the printer do the rest.

If you can't recruit any artistic volunteers, you can opt to resell cards from a fundraising company. Or you can find artists who might be willing to donate their services to your card project. For example, the Cottage Grove Humane Society in Oregon offers pet portrait cards that have been created by local artists who are members of the local art guild.

Level of...

- Difficulty = 🐾 🐾
- Planning Time = 🕐 🕐
- Upfront Costs = 💰 💰 💰
- Personnel = 👤 👤

75

Pet Artists

Feeling artsy? You don't have to leave the pets out. In fact, they can be the artists and you can put their paw-print and tail-wagging masterpieces up for sale! That's just what the Venango County Humane Society did with 26 of their best-behaved furry friends (and a lot of volunteers to mentor the critters' artistic endeavors). Dogs and even a few mellow cats strolled across canvases, leaving a trail of non-toxic paint to show their path. Some puppies even had their tail dipped in paint so they could wag it over a canvas in a feathery arc. Hilarious! (And very messy.)

Whether you choose a public venue or a private "studio" area like a backyard, be sure to have plenty of volunteers on hand to serve as walkers, handlers, and clean-up crew. Those furry paws can soak up a lot of paint.

Aside from using non-toxic substances, the only limit to the art you and your furry pals can create is your imagination. For sales purposes, you could create color schemes for local high schools and colleges, particularly if their teams are named the Bull Dogs or Tigers. After the big artistic event, you might consider converting the originals into prints, greeting cards, calendars, or other items for sale, as well.

Local artists and framing stores may give you a discount on matting and framing. The Vandango County Humane Society partnered with Transit Fine Arts Gallery to display their works and help with an art auction.

Level of...
- Difficulty = 🐾 🐾 🐾 🐾
- Planning Time = 🕐 🕐 🕐
- Upfront Costs = 💰 💰
- Personnel = 👤 👤 👤

76

Paw Prints for Sale

Selling paw prints is a simple way to solicit donations. If you've ever seen the donation shamrocks for the muscular dystrophy folks hanging in a store window, this idea is a variation on that theme. Instead of using shamrocks, you print paw prints on paper, to be purchased by donors and hung in a public place to show the donation has been made.

You can partner with a grocery, pet, or other high-traffic store and have the cashiers ask customers if they would like to purchase a paw print. For a small contribution of $1 or $2, they get their name (or their pet's name, if they prefer) on a paper paw print, which is put on display at the store for as long as the promotion runs.

Consider running the promotion around the winter holidays (when people are feeling generous), or in October, to celebrate National Adopt-A-Shelter-Dog Month. Or you can put your paw print in a heart shape for a valentine promotion.

Paw prints for contributions of $5, $10, or $20 could be larger or printed on different colored paper to reflect the amount donated.

Even if a customer doesn't donate, the name of your organization is prominently placed, which provides name recognition. One humane society that partnered with a grocery store earned more than $3,000 with this promotion.

Level of...

- Difficulty = 🐾
- Planning Time = 🕐
- Upfront Costs = 💰
- Personnel = 🧍

77

Pet Pageants

Nothing melts hearts, incites smiles and laughter and loosens purse strings more than pets in costume. Holding a pet costume pageant or parade is a fun way to advertise and fund your organization at the same time. Halloween, of course, lends itself to costumes, but don't forget Easter Parades or St. Patrick's Day. For the 4th of July, you can feature Patriotic Pets or Bathing Beasts for Summer Fun.

Once you have selected your pageant theme, find a public, animal-friendly area where you can hold your event, such as a park or school playground. (Be sure to check on permits and permissions.) Then get to work recruiting participants and advertising at schools, dog parks and pet stores. You can require participants pay a flat entrance fee (of $15 or so) or choose to have the participants fundraise on their own. In this case, set a minimum amount that is required in order to participate.

On the day of the event, dogs and pet owners can mingle and walk down a "cat walk." Invite pet vendors to showcase their pet products and add to the traffic. After the judges decide or the votes are tallied, award prizes such as sashes, plastic medals, dog biscuits and donated gift certificates for pet supplies. Have lots of prize categories so everyone feels included (Top Fundraiser, Best Costume, Best Canine/Human Pair, Silliest, Scariest, and so on).

Your event may start small, but could grow to be an annual affair. The "Bark in the Park" thrown by the Humane Society of Tampa Bay has grown into an "entertainment event" that includes not just a costume contest, but also a dog walk, agility competition, Easter egg hunt, and other events. In 2008, 1,500 participants and their pets helped raise a record $80,000 for the organization.

Level of...

- Difficulty = 🐾 🐾 🐾
- Planning Time = 🕐 🕐 🕐
- Upfront Costs = 💰 💰
- Personnel = 👤 👤 👤

78

Car Window Screens and Imprinted Products

Eye-catching fundraising products are a great way to attract attention and raise money. Items such as car window sun shields can provide education and advertising. The Seattle Animal Shelter sells a screen that reads, "If it's HOT enough to use your shade, save a life and leave your pets at home."

Other products that may help get the word out include coffee mugs, t-shirts, mouse pads or other office supplies. A number of online companies now offer imprinting services, so you can put your message on all types of things without having to order thousands at a time. Check out CafePress.com, PrintFection.com, or Shutterfly.com to get ideas for more products that your organization could sell. When you buy in small quantities, the unit cost can be high, so make sure that you can sell the item for a price that makes it worthwhile. (Consider the fact that retailers sell their items for at least double what they pay for them!)

Level of...

- Difficulty = 🐾 🐾 🐾
- Planning Time = 🕐 🕐
- Upfront Costs = 💰 💰 💰
- Personnel = 🧍 🧍

79

Meow Mixer

Building community is vital for any organization to be successful, so an informal networking event like a Meow Mixer or Doggie Hour is a good way to foster connections and conversation. If you find a friendly venue, it can become a weekly or monthly event, with a portion of the proceeds donated back to you.

If the location you find is amenable, you may want to bring some well-behaved mascots to the event to remind your sponsors and volunteers why your organization's work is so important. For instance, the Humane Society of Naples, Florida, brings a few kittens to their Meow Mixer. Bars and restaurants with large, open-air seating areas work best for people bringing dogs. You're happy because each donated "cover charge" goes directly to your organization, and the business owners are happy because they add another customer for the evening.

Level of...
- Difficulty = 🐾 🐾
- Planning Time = 🕐 🕐 🕐 🕐
- Upfront Costs = 💰 💰
- Personnel = 👤 👤

80

Pet Bingo

Bingo nights are a tried-and-true fundraiser for many organizations, providing both fun and funds. In fact, the Henry County Humane Society in Ohio is funded in large part by a licensed, Monday-night Bingo game. Many organizations such as churches and lodges already hold Bingo nights, so it's a good idea to check with them to see whether they would be willing to hold a benefit night for your group. If not, you can certainly ask them for tips on how to run your own. Serving or selling food like lemonade or cookies is always a good draw. You also can offer door prizes that have been donated to your organization.

If you do choose to hold your own event, be sure to check into gaming laws in your area. You may need special licenses for a public location. As a pet group, you already have a great theme song: "There was a farmer had a dog, and Bingo was his name...O!"

Level of...

- Difficulty = 🐾 🐾
- Planning Time = 🕐 🕐 🕐
- Upfront Costs = 💰 💰
- Personnel = 🧍 🧍 🧍

81

Add a "Donate" Button

Be sure to make it easy for anyone visiting your Web site to donate to your cause. If you don't have the resources to set up a secure server for credit card donations, add a button for credit card payments that links to a service like www.Propay.com or www.Paypal.com.

Signing up for these payment services is free, and they make it easy for a Web site visitor to make a donation with a credit card just by clicking a button. If you don't have the expertise to update your own site, ask around among your volunteers. Anyone who has experience with Web site design or development should be able to add a button to your site for a minimal charge. Then virtually anyone with an email address can use PayPal to donate. Plus, PayPal is owned by eBay and is particularly popular among eBay shoppers and sellers.

When visitors to your Web site see pictures of your animals up for adoption or read about the work you're doing in animal rescue, having an immediate way for them to respond and donate is crucial.

Level of...
- Difficulty = 🐾 🐾
- Planning Time = 🕐
- Upfront Costs = 💰
- Personnel = 💰

82

Partner with Parrotheads

If you're a Jimmy Buffet fan, you can partner with other Parrotheads in your area and chill out to some good tunage while raising money for your organization. That's what the Garland County Humane Society in Little Rock, Arkansas, does every year with its "Day Dreamin'" Fundraiser. The tagline for the event is "A License to Chill" and the humane society and Parrotheads make a weekend of it. There's a band Friday evening at a local hotel sports bar, another band plays poolside on Saturday, and the finale on Sunday is in the hotel ballroom. People can see all three bands for one cover charge, which also includes a silent auction and raffle during the party amidst all the margaritas and tunes.

The fundraiser is a lot of fun and showcases a key fundraising principle. If you can combine your passions, do it! Work with other groups to create the kind of event you'd like to attend yourself. If pets aren't your only passion, bring others in on the fun. The more connections and crossovers in your life, the better for you and the better for your organization's bottom line.

Level of...
- Difficulty = 🐾 🐾 🐾 🐾
- Planning Time = 🕐 🕐 🕐 🕐
- Upfront Costs = 💰 💰 💰 💰
- Personnel = 👤 👤 👤 👤

83

Pennies from Heaven

Savvy fundraisers know that spare change adds up! An easy way to collect donations is by distributing cans to local stores and restaurants for a "Pennies from Heaven" campaign (or "Raining Cats and Dogs" if your focus in on spaying and neutering).

If you don't have the resources to monitor many can locations, you can set a goal amount, such as 1 million pennies, or a time limit for the promotion, such as one month. Creating the cans is easy. You can make them out of pet food cans, coffee cans or other recycled materials.

The key is to have an opening on the top with a slot, so people can put money in easily (but not take it out). You should keep the cans in extremely visible locations, such as right next to the cash register. If it's possible to affix the can to something large and difficult to move, that's even better. The more eye-catching and creative you can be with your collection mechanism, the better.

Another way to collect change is to distribute collection cans or boxes to local schools, so the kids can carry them home. UNICEF's Halloween collection boxes are based on this principle.

A little donation box sitting on a dresser for a week can accumulate quite a bit of spare change. When combined with many other boxes sitting on many other people's dressers, all those coins can help a lot of animals.

Level of...

- Difficulty = 🐾 🐾 🐾
- Planning Time = 🕐 🕐 🕐
- Upfront Costs = 💰 💰
- Personnel = 🚹 🚹 🚹

84

Bow Wow Beauties

Think you have the prettiest puppy? Think Miss America can't compete with your cat? Put it to the test and raise some money for your organization with a pet beauty pageant.

Participants pay an entrance fee to walk their critters down the catwalk and compete in categories such as eveningwear, swimwear, casual attire, talent (maybe Frisbee catch, singing/howling or agility) or contests like best manners or longest tail.

You need a pet-friendly location and lots of advertising so you can draw all the "pet people" in your community. The Heartland Humane Society of Corvallis, Oregon, held a "Bow Wow Beauty Pageant" and pet walk/run on a Saturday in a local park. Registration for the walk was $20, which included entry into the beauty pageant. Those who opted not to walk could enter the beauty pageant for $5. The humane society also included a "clever canine contest." Prizes were awarded for longest tongue, best kisser and pet/owner look-alike.

If you can combine your beauty pageant with demonstrations and events like agility, you can showcase both how pretty and how talented your critters are.

Level of...
- Difficulty = 🐾 🐾 🐾
- Planning Time = 🕐 🕐 🕐 🕐
- Upfront Costs = 💰 💰 💰
- Personnel = 👤 👤 👤

85

Microchipping

Microchipping is a great way to reunite pets with their owners, but it also can be a fundraising opportunity as well. You can focus on educating people on responsible pet ownership and make money at the same time.

The Humane Society of Southern Arizona in Tucson holds a microchip clinic offering a microchip and a quality identification tag at discount for a limited time. During the promotion, the humane society charges just $10 for the microchip, $2 for a small tag, and $4 for a large tag.

In Pittsfield, Massachusetts, the Berkshire Humane Society combines a microchip clinic with rabies vaccinations. They charge $25 for the microchipping and $10 for a three-year rabies vaccine.

You'll need to send out press releases and let as many people know about the event as possible. If you are new to microchipping, be sure to check with veterinarians in your area for more information on the type of chips they are using and rules that may apply in your area.

Level of...
- Difficulty = 🐾 🐾
- Planning Time = 🕐 🕐 🕐 🕐
- Upfront Costs = 💰 💰 💰
- Personnel = 👤 👤 👤

86

Pet-Friendly Plant Sale

Plant sales are a great spring fundraiser for your organization. Talk to local nurseries and florists about plant donations. You can also ask your volunteers to grow seedlings or dig up plants from their own yard and plant them in attractive pots. Tomato plants and herbs are great sellers. On the day of the sale, be sure to have enough cash on hand for giving appropriate change, a large donation jar for extra donations and some small foodstuffs for sale as well. Gardeners are always looking for ways to spruce up their garden and this way their purchases go to a good cause.

The Nebraska Humane Society partners with the Canoyer Garden Center every year for its plant sale. The Canoyer Garden Center creates special combinations of plants just for the event, with arrangements for full sun to shady areas. They also sell hanging baskets, decorated pots and planters.

The plant sale provides an opportunity for education on plants that may be poisonous to pets. Go the ASPCA Web site (www.ASPCA.org), get their list of common poisonous plants, and share the information with attendees.

Level of...
- Difficulty = 🐾 🐾
- Planning Time = 🕐 🕐 🕐
- Upfront Costs = 💰 💰
- Personnel = 🧍 🧍 🧍

87

Blind Auction

A blind auction is a fun way to raise funds for your group. It works best as part of an ongoing event such as a regular luncheon or dinner meeting. You ask each event attendee to bring a wrapped package. The contents can be an amusing "gag" gift or something of actual value.

Use this as a type of "white elephant" or "re-gifting" gift exchange. Think of the possibilities—you can raise money for a worthy cause and get rid of that ugly weird thing that's been lurking in the back of the closet! A creative donor can weight his box with a brick to disguise the contents or use an oversize box for a very small present. Some people add anticipation by wrapping boxes within boxes. You get the idea; the goal is to make the gift-giving fun and full of surprises!

You will need one really good donation that works as the "carrot" to entice people to participate. Announce that at least one of the boxes contains a high-denomination bill or a donated travel certificate. You should choose something of value that is small enough to fit in any box.

As the guests arrive, they place their boxes on a display table so potential bidders can examine them and speculate on the contents. Whether you use a live or silent auction, make sure everyone has time to pick up and shake the boxes before they bid. (Guessing what's inside is part of the fun!)

At the specified time, auction all the boxes. You can have either a silent or live auction. If it's a live auction, make sure you auction off some *good* prizes at first to stimulate more bidding. Above all, make sure you leave enough time at the end for people to open their box in front of the group. Done well, a blind auction can be a great source of laughter and a few extra funds, too.

Level of...

- Difficulty = 🐾 🐾 🐾
- Planning Time = 🕐 🕐 🕐
- Upfront Costs = 💰 💰 💰
- Personnel = 🧍 🧍 🧍

88

Knitted or Crocheted Items

If you or your volunteers have a crafty side, consider putting your knitting, crocheting or sewing skills to use as part of a fundraiser. Volunteers donate their time and supplies to create one-of-a-kind people- and pet-wear that you can sell.

Baby booties are always a popular seller for the small human set. When it comes to pet-wear, you can offer items like shih tzu sweaters and corgi cardigans to promote both the clothing and your furry models that are up for adoption. You can approach local knitting and sewing clubs to see if they'd like to put things they have made out for sale for you.

Another way to use knitting and sewing is to get sponsorship for the items that are created. For instance, for every blanket square or quilt block created within a certain amount of time, sponsors might donate a specified amount of money. This type of quilt-a-thon or knit-a-thon can be a great way to work with crafters in your community.

The Seattle Humane Society encouraged its crafty volunteers to make supplies, as well. As part of its Cat Cuddles Knitting Project, volunteers knit small blankets, so adoptable cats have something cozy and cuddly in their cubby. The cat blankets are machine washable and measure about 14" x 16", so they are quick and easy to make.

Level of...

- Difficulty = 🐾 🐾
- Planning Time = 🕐 🕐
- Upfront Costs = 💰
- Personnel = 👤 👤

89

Appraise for Strays

Everyone hopes that they have priceless treasures in the attic. A fun fundraiser is to work with local antique dealers who review and evaluate these items. Basically, you put on your own version of "Antique Roadshow," but in this case, it's more like "Appraise for Strays!"

For a small donation, participants can have their china, coins, books, paintings, jewelry, furniture and odd, dusty doo-dads appraised by professional appraisers. It's important that you find reputable people to do the expert valuations. You really don't want your participants misled about the worth of their family heirlooms.

Beyond that, you just need to find a location, set a time and, of course, advertise the event. You can talk not only to local antique stores, but also to your local historical society. Some of the items may have historical value, so the historical society could partner with you on the event.

It's great if you can work your appraisal fundraiser in with another larger event. For example, the Galveston Island Humane Society runs an "Antique Roadshow" as part of its Home and Garden show. A local appraiser is on hand to appraise pieces brought to the show and to help people learn how to spot authentic antiques.

Level of...

- Difficulty = 🐾 🐾 🐾
- Planning Time = 🕐 🕐 🕐 🕐
- Upfront Costs = 💰 💰 💰
- Personnel = 🧍 🧍 🧍

90

Benefactor Auction

If you have supporters who are looking to downsize, ask if they are willing to auction their pieces as a benefit for your organization. That's what a 90-year-old benefactor of Payson Humane Society did in the summer of 2007.

Kitty Lucek (known locally as Miss Kitty) had been involved with the Payson Humane Society since its organization. She had been trying to sell some of her belongings on her own, but instead decided to have an auction and give the money to the humane society's building fund. Another couple opted to contribute more than a half-dozen truckloads of items left from an estate sale. With the combined donations, it was quite an auction; filled with unusual items like a parking meter, an old brass change maker, antique furniture, and vintage linens.

The next time you hear someone say, "I have to get rid of all this stuff!" ask them how they plan to do it. You never know when a fundraising opportunity is going to land right in your lap. So when it does, get the word out and make the most of it!

Level of...

- Difficulty = 🐾 🐾 🐾 🐾
- Planning Time = 🕐 🕐 🕐
- Upfront Costs = 💰 💰
- Personnel = 🧍 🧍 🧍

91

Business Donation Day

Teaming up with a business and having a "percentage of sales" donation day is a great way to raise funds. The business you team with benefits from the extra traffic and goodwill generated by the event and you have a partner that can help with advertising and staffing. Your partner business may be willing to offer special incentives and discounts as part of the event. Having someone there with a donation jar for those who aren't shopping is a good idea, too.

Every year in Phoenix, Arizona, the Mane Attraction Make-up and Hair Salon holds "Beauty to the RESCUE," which is a fundraiser for RESCUE, an Arizona animal organization. Salon personnel volunteer their talent for the human population, offering reduced-price haircuts and other services. In recent years, a mobile groomer has also set up shop to tend to the canine crowd. The event has become so popular that people line up starting at 9:00 a.m. Since 2001, the event has raised more than $100,000 for the rescue group.

Level of...
- Difficulty = 🐾 🐾 🐾
- Planning Time = 🕐 🕐 🕐
- Upfront Costs = 💰 💰
- Personnel = 👤 👤 👤

92

Bring Your Dog to Work

"Take Your Dog to Work Day" rolls around every June. Pet Sitters International created this holiday to celebrate the fact that dogs are great companions—even at work! The holiday encourages people to adopt from shelters and rescues, so you can ride the coattails of this national publicity by working with local businesses to do your own "Take Your Dog to Work Day" fundraiser.

To get involved in the fun, you can visit www.TakeYourDog. com and download a free copy of PSI's "Guide to Taking Your Dog to Work." The guide contains a number of tips to help you work with participating local businesses.

In fact, PSI suggests that businesses "Ask your local shelter or favorite rescue group to join your TYDTW Day event. Invite them to bring adoptable pets or information about local adoption opportunities to your place of business. Consider holding a fundraiser to benefit the guest shelter."

PSI's promotional efforts mean that businesses are already predisposed to talk to you! Take advantage of that fact and talk to your volunteers in the spring about getting involved. Some may work for a business that would be willing to participate. It's a fun way to celebrate the human-animal bond, showcase your animals and raise a few bucks at the same time.

Level of...

- Difficulty = 🐾 🐾
- Planning Time = 🕐 🕐 🕐
- Upfront Costs = 💰 💰
- Personnel = 🧍 🧍

93

Super Scooper Day

Here's an idea that's a variation on the classic "leaf-raking" fundraiser. (In the fall, you go to homes with trees in the yard and give the homeowner a flyer that explains that you are raising money by raking leaves for a fee.)

You can take this approach and make it more "dog-friendly" by having a "Super Scooper Day" fundraiser. Advertise that on a specific day, the Scoop Patrol will available to clean up the 'hood. Make sure you come equipped with lots of scoops, disposal bags and so forth, so you can take away and properly dispose of what you scoop up.

You can do flyers and/or radio and newspaper advertising. Slogans like "Stuff Happens and We're Here to Clean It Up" never fail to amuse those who will gladly give you a donation to let you do the dirty work for a change!

Level of...

- Difficulty = 🐾 🐾
- Planning Time = 🕐 🕐
- Upfront Costs = 💰 💰
- Personnel = 🧍 🧍 🧍

94

Condolence Cards

One of the saddest things about owning a pet is the fact that they don't live as long as we humans do. Eventually, many owners are faced with the prospect of euthanizing a dog or cat. Veterinarians dread this sad occasion and some want to do something to express their sympathy. A number of years ago a veterinarian in Idaho approached the local animal shelter about donating money when he had to euthanize one of his pet patients.

The shelter helped design a condolence card, which was sent to the owner. It said that the veterinarian had made a donation to the animal shelter in the name of the pet.

Many people find some comfort in helping other homeless animals after they have lost a pet and will make donations in their pet's name. Be sure to recognize this generosity in some way, either in your newsletter or by sending a card or letter. You may want to find or create "Rainbow Bridge" cards or other appropriate pet loss cards to send when you receive this type of donation.

Level of...

- Difficulty = 🐾 🐾
- Planning Time = 🕐 🕐
- Upfront Costs = 💰 💰
- Personnel = 🧍

95

Bakeless Bake Sale

Anyone who has been the recipient of Aunt Agatha's famous rum and gelatin fruitcake knows that some foodstuffs are a harder sell than others. A great way to avoid the selling aspect of a bake sale is to throw a Bakeless Bake Sale. Similar to the no-show party fundraiser, a bakeless bake sale involves *no* recipes, *no* shopping for ingredients, *no* chopping, *no* measuring, *no*baking, *no* hot kitchen, *no* dirty dishes, *no* decorating, *no* wrapping, *no* pricing and *no*staffing of a sale table in the heat/cold/rain/snow.

Instead, send an invitation highlighting all the advantages of *not* having a bake sale (see above). Suggest donation amounts for items. For example, "it's worth $20 for me *not* to bake six dozen brownies." In your invitation, be sure to list the bakeless bake sale date, so you have a deadline for donations. This fundraiser is a great, low-cost way to encourage people to donate to your organization and an opportunity for you to give them a smile.

Level of...
- Difficulty = 🐾
- Planning Time = 🕐
- Upfront Costs = 💰
- Personnel = 🧍

96

Lock Up Someone

A fun fundraiser is to throw someone in the doghouse! Locking someone in a doghouse, kennel, or shelter for a specific amount of time, or until you reach your goal, generates a lot of local press, particularly if the person is a well-known celebrity such as a television or radio personality. You can have updates on your Web site (Free Him Now—Donate Now!). Or you can make it a ransom situation. ("We won't let him go until we can feed 100 dogs for a year!")

A lock up can be a very successful and popular event. Two DJs in Colorado—Bill Cody and Ted Rose—along with Bill's dog Bo, broadcast live from a dog kennel for three day to raise money for the Humane Society of Weld County. The "Cause for Paws" accepted donations of money, food, cleaning supplies, blankets, puppy and kitten formula, bottles, and other supplies. Bill and Ted (yes, they called it their Excellent Adventure) and Bo had participated in a similar event the previous year, which raised more than $100,000.

Level of...

- Difficulty = 🐾 🐾 🐾 🐾
- Planning Time = 🕐 🕐 🕐 🕐
- Upfront Costs = 💰 💰 💰
- Personnel = 👤 👤 👤

97

Mystery Dinner

A Murder Mystery Dinner Party event is a somewhat elaborate, yet fun way to raise money. It's also the type of thing that can garner a tremendous amount of press and word- of-mouth advertising. If all goes well, people may talk about it for years.

The easiest way to hold one of these events is to obtain a "Dinner and a Murder Mystery Game" from www.DinnerAndA Murder.com or another "mystery kit." Try to avoid using an overly scripted game. Instead go for a "mingle" format, which makes the game interactive. Then you can play the same game with the same players and each time it is different.

You'll need to determine where to hold the event and how many people you will invite, work out a budget, and set a ticket price. You could include "add-on" fundraisers during the event, such as a silent auction or extra (paid) desserts and/or drinks.

The Fox Valley Humane Association held a mystery dinner inviting guests to help solve the kidnapping of an opera-singing golden retriever named Basso Profundo Pooch. The event raised more than $25,000 for the shelter.

Level of...
- Difficulty = 🐾 🐾 🐾 🐾
- Planning Time = 🕐 🕐 🕐 🕐
- Upfront Costs = 💰 💰 💰 💰
- Personnel = 👤 👤 👤 👤

98

Paws Across the Water Duck Race

Bring out the competitive spirit of your donors and stage a rubber duck race! That's exactly what the Humane Society of North Myrtle Beach has done for the last three years with its annual Paws Across the Water Duck Race. More than ten thousand yellow rubber ducks are dropped into the Intracoastal Waterway at Barefoot Landing. Each duck has been "adopted" by someone for a small donation. Ducks are numbered and correspond to the adopters. The first duck to reach the bridge wins its adopter a spa package. It's become an annual event, with vendors along the shore watching the progress. After all, who doesn't want to see 10,000 rubber duckies floating by?

Imaginative fundraisers like this one are a great way to generate press and create community. Maybe the Intracoastal Waterway doesn't run through your area, but think about other ways that you can capitalize on the particular flavor of your community.

Level of...
- Difficulty = 🐾 🐾 🐾 🐾
- Planning Time = 🕐 🕐 🕐
- Upfront Costs = 💰 💰 💰
- Personnel = 👤 👤 👤 👤

99

Artwork Contest

If you want to sell anything from t-shirts to posters or decide it's time for a new logo, consider having an art contest. People pay a donation to enter the contest and in the end, one lucky (and talented) winner has his or her work showcased by your organization.

Alternatively, you might go to galleries and ask the owners if any of their artists are animal lovers. Many times artists will donate their time to create artwork if they know you will do a quality job of reproducing it on the item(s) you are going to sell. Always credit the artist and acknowledge his or her contribution. If the artist has local or national name recognition, having his or her name on the item will help it fly off the shelves.

You also could have an art contest in the schools. Kids love to draw, so give them an opportunity to express their creativity! If you are getting printed materials such as posters done, ask a printer to discount the price of printing. Then be sure to give the printer credit for the donation in your promotional materials!

Level of...

- Difficulty = 🐾 🐾 🐾
- Planning Time = 🕐 🕐
- Upfront Costs = 💰 💰
- Personnel = 🧍 🧍

100

Links of Life

A "Links of Life" fundraiser is a good way to make a point and raise money at the same time. For this fundraiser, you sell strips of paper to make a paper chain.

Each link in the chain represents an animal that is euthanized during a given time, an animal that is in a shelter needing a home, an animal born because one animal wasn't spayed or neutered, or something else you want the public to know.

The Legacy Boxer Rescue in Texas sold links for one dollar each. They determined that 10,300 dog and cats had been euthanized in June 2006 in shelters in the Texas counties of Dallas, Denton, Tarrant and Collin. They created exactly 10,300 colored paper links. As they sold the strips, they asked people to write a message on the paper, such as "Please Spay or Neuter" or "in Memory of Spot."

As they said in the promotional flyer, "The chain will be nothing short of spectacular when it is displayed. The colors are endless, but it is very sobering to know that each one of these links represents a cat or dog who lost their life because there simply were not enough homes."

Level of...

- Difficulty = 🐾 🐾 🐾
- Planning Time = 🕐 🕐
- Upfront Costs = 💰 💰
- Personnel = 👤 👤

101

Letter Writing Campaign

The last fundraising idea in our list of 101 is a return to the basics: write and ask for a donation. Letter writing campaigns can be immensely successful. A professional writer (preferably one who will donate his time) can craft a moving letter. Alternatively, many sample appeal letters that can be modified are available online. Be sure that the letter conveys the importance of the work you do for the animals, the people who love them, and the community at large.

Don't underestimate the importance of pictures and layout. Fido and Fluffy with their happy smiles might make the difference between a good appeal and a great one. Personal stories can be particularly moving. As a rescue professional, you're likely to have amazing stories about how animals can transform people's lives or how pets have overcome difficult circumstances and found happy homes. Before you mail your letter, be sure to have several people read the final copy to check for typos.

Another advantage to letter writing is that the expense is minimal. Following the US Postal Service's bulk mailing rules can cut your expenses even more, assuming you have a large enough mailing list.

Letter campaigns are a reminder of how important it is to keep a contact list of previous contributors and adopters. Never forget about those people who believe in the work you do. They are among your most important resources!

Level of...

- Difficulty =
- Planning Time =
- Upfront Costs =
- Personnel =

Index

P

About the Author
Susan Daffron

Susan Daffron is the founder of the National Association of Pet Rescue Professionals (www.naprp.com), which provides tools and information to help humane organizations save more companion animal lives. She also is the president of Logical Expressions, Inc., a book and software publishing company in Sandpoint, Idaho. She has authored 11 books including *Happy Hound: Develop a Great Relationship with Your Adopted Dog or Puppy* and *Happy Tabby: Develop a Great Relationship with Your Adopted Cat or Kitten.*

Two months after she and her husband moved to Idaho, Susan started volunteering at the local animal shelter. Her first week there, she adopted a sickly black puppy named Leia and nursed her back to health. She adopted two more dogs from the shelter and later adopted another dog from a rescue group in California and a cat from another local shelter.

Susan volunteered and subsequently worked as an employee and board member at the animal shelter for four years. Over the time she was involved, she used her graphic design and writing background to dramatically increase the visibility of the shelter in the community. She created hundreds of promotional materials, including banners, brochures, Web sites, forms, flyers, press releases, a new quarterly membership newsletter, and helped organize many fundraising events.

Susan also worked as a part-time veterinary technician at a low-cost spay/neuter clinic. There she learned more about veterinary issues, researched grants, and helped with software and administration issues.

A recognized expert on Web, editorial, design, and publishing topics, Susan has been involved in publishing since the late 80s.

About the National Association of Pet Rescue Professionals

The National Association of Pet Rescue Professionals is a membership association made up of people who are working for animal shelters, humane societies or rescue groups.

You can choose from free or paid membership:

1. **FREE "Helping Paw" members** receive a free report, weekly newsletter, and live access to monthly expert teleseminars.

2. **Along with the newsletter and teleseminars, with your paid "Golden Paw Insider" membership** you gain access to the private membership area of the NAPRP Web site, which has information and tools you need to save more pet's lives! You receive tangible benefits in three important areas:

- **Adopter Education**: two printed books for adopted pet owners, 100+ customizable articles, and more.

- **Fundraising and Promotion**: fundraising ideas specific to humane and rescue groups, information on grants and grant writing, fundraising worksheets, templates for marketing materials, graphics, and more.

- **Administration and Management**: customizable business forms for tasks like faxes, telephone messages, volunteer management, and more.

The easiest way to learn more about the National Association of Pet Rescue Professionals is to visit us online at **www.naprp.com**

Share Funds to the Rescue with a Friend

If you like this book, share it with your fundraising friends!

Please send me:

Qty	Title	Price	Total
	Funds to the Rescue	$19.95	
	Shipping & Handling - $5.50 for first book, $1.00 for each additional book for US Priority Mail within the U.S.*		

_____ Check enclosed with order

_____ Please charge my credit card [   ] Visa   [   ] Master Card

Number: _____

Name on Card: _____ Exp. Date: _____

Buyer's Name:_____

Buyer's Address: _____

Shipping Address (if different):_____

_____

Please mail with your payment to:

Logical Expressions, Inc.,

311 Fox Glen Road, Sandpoint, ID 83864

* *Please contact us for more information on orders mailed outside of the U.S. (Our number is 208-265-6147)*